PRAISE FOR 'THE N

Sam Harris, author of the New York Times bestsellers The End of Faith, Letter to a Christian Nation, The Moral Landscape, and Free Will:

"Most people are completely taken in by the illusion of free will. Happily, Richard Oerton is not among them. The Nonsense of Free Will is a wonderfully clear – and very clever – little book."

Professor Ted Honderich, Grote Professor Emeritus of the Philosophy of Mind and Logic, University College London:

"There are philosophical, scientific, scholarly, novel, determined, American, pompous, dotty and other books on free will and determinism. There are also a few books that are lucid and informal introductions for ordinary readers and let you know that your free will does not exist. Richard Oerton's may be the best of these."

Joshua Rozenberg, lawyer and legal commentator, formerly legal editor of the Daily Telegraph:

"This book is superbly written and a delight to read. Starting as a clearly reasoned treatment of determinism, it merges seamlessly into a critique of English criminal law and penal policy, and ends with a plea for society to abandon what the author sees as its irrational belief in free will."

Dr. Stephen Cretney, D.C.L., F.B.A., Q.C., LL.D., Emeritus Fellow of All Souls College, Oxford, formerly Professor and Dean of the Faculty of Law at Bristol University, and a Law Commissioner from 1978 to 1983:

"This fascinating book explains and discusses one of the most difficult questions underlying criminal liability – are we right to work on the basis that all sane people can exercise 'free will'? Richard Oerton explores the free will v. determinism debate with remarkable and rare clarity. This is not a book only for academics: it is of vital interest to all who want to think about the way society is organised."

THE
NONSENSE
OF
FREE WILL

FACING UP TO A FALSE BELIEF

RICHARD OERTON

Matador
9 Priory Business Park,
Wistow Road, Kibworth Beauchamp,
Leicestershire. LE8 0RX
Tel: (+44) 116 279 2299
Fax: (+44) 116 279 2277
Email: books@troubador.co.uk
Web: www.troubador.co.uk/matador

ISBN 978 1780882 871

British Library Cataloguing in Publication Data.
A catalogue record for this book is available from the British Library.

Typeset in 11pt Bembo by Troubador Publishing Ltd, Leicester, UK
Printed and bound in the UK by TJ International, Padstow, Cornwall

Matador is an imprint of Troubador Publishing Ltd

This book is dedicated

to my grandchildren, Lily and Grace,
Eve and Gabriel, and Louis Jacob

and

to the memory of Louis Jacob's father,
James Oerton,
forensic clinical psychologist

"I often have long conversations all by myself, and I am so clever that sometimes I don't understand a single word of what I am saying."

"Then you should certainly lecture on Philosophy", said the Dragonfly, and he spread a pair of lovely gauze wings and soared away into the sky.

Oscar Wilde, *The Remarkable Robot,*
from *The Happy Prince and other stories,*
first published in 1888.

Contents

Preface

What do we talk about when we talk about free will? A recent book which touches on this subject says, "Tell most people they don't have free will, and they will defiantly tell you you're wrong" [1]. I guess this is true. But I think it's true also that if you were to ask them to explain what exactly it is that they claim to have when they claim to have free will, they would flounder. While I was writing this book I asked one of my grand-daughters, who happened at the time to be studying an aspect of Roman history for her A levels, what she understood by the term "free will". She answered kindly but firmly, "Oh no, Grandad: I'll tell you anything you want to know about the Catiline conspiracy, but not free will." It seemed a wise reply.

If this book has a main theme, then this is it. Free will is indefinable, and it's indefinable because it is an incoherent idea – a nonsense, literally a piece of non-sense. If free will were a comprehensible concept, the job of a free will denier would be to examine it with a view to showing why, despite its comprehensibility, it doesn't exist, or doesn't exist in human beings. In fact, however, my purpose is rather to show that it is not a comprehensible concept at all, but a self-contradictory one, so that it is intrinsically incapable of any existence.

Attempts to define free will seem to resolve themselves into definitions of an absence. Free will is what exists if something else does not exist. In its popular conception - the only conception which will bear the weight we put on it - free will is what exists in the absence of determinism. (As we shall see later, this isn't the conception advanced by "compatibilist" philosophers, though even they conceive it in terms of an absence - in their case, an absence of external compulsion or mental illness.) But this sort of negative definition is not acceptable. I suppose you can define peace, rather crudely, as an absence of war, or war as an absence of peace, but you can say much more than that about war and peace: you can, if pressed to do so, explain more or less what constitutes the one and what constitutes the other. Not so with free will.

The nearest you can get, and the nearest I could get in this book, to defining free will is to show, by means of examples, the effects which its exercise is supposedly capable of producing. Whatever else is true of our idea of free will, it must be true that, if we possess it, we really might have acted in ways different from the ways in which we did act. Because of free will, Hitler really might have shown particular benevolence towards the Jews, spoken disparagingly of the Aryan race, and insisted that Germans already had more *lebensraum* than they knew what to do with [2]. And since free will must mean not only that people might do good things instead of bad, but equally that they might do bad things instead of good, Nelson Mandela and F.W. de Klerk, instead of acting in such a way as to win themselves a Nobel Peace Prize, really might have conspired together to plunge the whole of South Africa into civil war. And my grand-daughter, instead of responding in the way she did, might have said to herself, "Poor old sod, I don't know what he's on about but, preoccupied though I am with thoughts of Cicero and Catilina, I'll try to answer his question", and attempted (perhaps without much success) to do so. And these things might have happened - really *might* have happened, might *really* have happened - despite the whole history of the universe and the way in which that history produced, formed and bore upon the individual people concerned up to the moment when they did what they did and didn't do what they didn't do.

We'll say no more about my grand-daughter (so goodbye, Eve), but the idea that Hitler, Mandela and de Klerk might really have behaved in the ways suggested in the last paragraph is so implausible that most people would reject it out of hand. Where does that leave them? It is at this point that many would seek refuge in some sort of compromise. Some might say that our free will consists in the ability to make the best of the hand which history (in the shape of our heredity and our past environment) has dealt us; but of course this ability, its nature and strength, must itself be a part of that same hand and so, come to that, must be our conception of what "the best" is. Other people, while reluctantly accepting that complete free will is impossible, might still want to assert that some (incomplete) free will must exist somehow, or somewhere; but, as I hope to show in the book, a belief of this kind would be of no practical utility even if it were tenable.

The fact that free will is conceived negatively, as what exists in the absence of determinism, has at least two ill consequences. The first, as I've mentioned, is that little attempt is ever made to give the concept any positive definition of its own, so that the impossibility of framing such a definition goes unnoticed. The second is the widespread belief, held even by some philosophers, that all you have to do in order to preserve and uphold free will is to pick holes in determinism. But even if such holes can be picked - even if, for example, an element of real chance, real indeterminacy, enters into human behaviour - this would not serve to establish free will unless free will is itself a meaningful concept.

This book contains quite a few references to philosophers, but I am a lawyer, not a philosopher, and I didn't conceive it as a book of philosophy. I certainly haven't tried to adopt or regurgitate the views of any philosopher. I set out to write almost an anti-philosophical book; a "come on, get real, cut the crap and just *look* at this" sort of book; very nearly a "this isn't philosophy, this is common sense" sort of book. My intention, above all, was to bring the subject down to earth, in the hope that people who may know nothing of philosophy, but are open to reason and willing to think for themselves, will see the nonsensicality of what we call free will. Whether I've succeeded is not for me to judge, but I think the attempt is worthwhile. Our belief in free will is a false belief and we are better off without false beliefs because any false belief enslaves us even if it goes by a name which has the word "free" in it.

1.

Introductory

I can remember the moment when I became a determinist. It was well over half a century ago and I was fourteen or fifteen years old. I was sitting in a classroom at school. Either the lesson had finished or it hadn't started, or perhaps it was taking place but I was paying no attention to it. And whatever train of thought I was idly pursuing led me to see, suddenly and without warning, that I was inescapably the product of a complex chain of cause and effect stretching back into the past and ultimately to a time before I was born, and that because I was a product of this chain so, too, were my thoughts and feelings and actions. In my mind's eye I saw existence as something like a patterned carpet slowly unrolling, its size unimaginably great and its pattern unimaginably complex. The part of it which has already unrolled is the past, the pattern now exposed but most of it lost beyond recollection. The part still rolled up is the future, and although its pattern is not yet visible it is already fixed because it follows ineluctably from the pattern of the earlier part. My own life was a tiny piece of the pattern located just where the carpet was unrolling, part visible, part not, its shape and nature determined by the fact that it fitted into the larger pattern beside and behind it.

I think that I imagined myself the first person to have had this insight. In fact, of course, the arguments between determinists and proponents of free will have their origins long ago. It has been said that each generation – or each generation of budding philosophers – discovers these arguments anew. But although each generation rediscovers them and dances around them, no real consensus ever emerges from their activity. They are like a large family playing a long-lasting board game like Monopoly and enjoying it so much that they want it never to end. This struck me, when I first discovered it, as deeply strange. It isn't as if the outcome of the arguments doesn't matter: in some important ways, as I hope to show, it matters very much. Yet, desultorily, at an abstruse level and inconclusively, the arguments go on. As I read more about them, I found myself lost in wonder at the sophistry with which the issues were treated or, much more often it seemed to me, avoided. I came to see determinism as an elephant in the room – something which is both obvious and significant but which no one wants to acknowledge. I realised in the end that the reasons for this are not so difficult to understand, but that is something to explore later on.

In describing my first awareness of determinism I have used a visual metaphor: the patterned carpet. To "understand" something must always, I suspect, be in some sense to picture it visually. It is no accident that someone to whom something eventually becomes clear will say, "Oh, I see", or, "Oh, *now* I see". It is somehow pictured in the mind's eye. And if it is never pictured in this way then no argument in its favour, no proof of its existence, will ever be convincing or perhaps even comprehensible. I have become aware of this, more than once, in discussing determinism with other people. If you can imagine a seaside penny-in-the-slot machine in which what you see through the butler's eyes is determinism, then it's clear that you won't see it unless and until the penny drops. And this is so often the problem with trying to convey the *idea* of determinism, and the incoherence of free will: there is a penny that doesn't drop.

As time passed, I came to express my own vision of determinism in two linked propositions: *a person acts as he does because he is what he is; and he has not made himself what he is.* (This was at a time of political incorrectness and that must be my only excuse for having made no explicit reference to the female sex.) For me, these propositions still sum up determinism - or, perhaps more accurately, the incoherence of free will - and I'm still a bit surprised that anyone disagrees with either of them. I'm still more surprised by people who don't disagree with them but still don't "see" determinism. For them, it seems to me, the penny just hasn't dropped.

For most of my life I have thought that the question whether human behaviour was produced by determinism, or by free will, was a philosophical question and that a philosophical question was a question so difficult that only a trained philosopher could handle it – with the corollary that since I wasn't a trained philosopher I couldn't handle it. Old age has made me impatient with this view. Some of the questions with which philosophers concern themselves don't seem to have much bearing on everyday existence. One thinks of the mathematics don who raised his glass at a university function with the words, "Here's to pure mathematics, and may it never be of the slightest use to anyone." To many people, philosophical questions seem like that – abstract and abstruse, technical and having little to do with real life. That philosophical questions are thought of in this way, and that "free will or determinism" is thought of as a philosophical question, may be one reason why few people bother their heads with it. But this particular question does matter and it does have implications for everyday life, and it doesn't seem to me that there is anything very technical or abstruse about it.

But what is a philosophical question anyway? Professor Ted Honderich, a modern philosopher, who happens to be a leading determinist though that's irrelevant for present purposes, points out that what distinguishes philosophers is not so much the questions with which they concern themselves, because these are likely to fall within the purview of other branches of science or learning [3]. What distinguishes philosophers is their *approach* to the questions: as he puts it [4], "Good thinking in getting a clear hold. That is the real impulse of philosophy." And surely it is an impulse to which anyone may be subject, and to which anyone can respond. In the case of this particular question, it seems to me, they may do so successfully.

So frustration forms a large part of my motivation for trying to write this book. I think determinism matters. I think it's something which has been shuttled off to professional philosophers when it isn't really a philosophical problem at all. I even think sometimes that most people's wilful blindness to its implications leads to a lot of cruelty and is quite a blot on our civilisation, and that civilisation's next step forward must involve us in accepting them. And after a lifetime's acquaintance with the question, I want to make a last attempt to convey it, to explain it, to get it across, to let it be seen.

PART I

DETERMINISM AND FREE WILL

2.

What is determinism?

One afternoon, when I was a small boy, I was taken to the park. I felt the wind blowing and saw the trees swaying, and I decided that the trees' movements were causing the wind. When I voiced this conclusion I was told that it was the other way about, but it took me quite some time to accept that I was wrong.

The idea of cause and effect – the knowledge that if something happens it must have been caused by something else, that one thing leads to another – is fundamental to human beings. How could we possibly live our lives without it? We should have no idea how to explain a past event or to bring about a future one. Why would we seek the cause of an illness if illnesses were uncaused or seek cures if cures had no effect? If, that afternoon in the park, feeling the wind and seeing the trees, the small boy got cause and effect the wrong way round, his mistake is less significant than his almost instinctive grasp of the concept of causality – of the fact that phenomena *have* causal explanations. It is this intuitive grasp which, to children, justifies their incessant search for these explanations – their demand for answers to the question, "Why?", their irritating habit of greeting one answer to this question only with a repetition of the same question.

And this is the essence of determinism, because determinism is causality.

Suppose that you decide to make yourself a cup of tea. You turn on the kitchen tap and the water flows into the kettle. What causes

7

the water to flow? You could say, the turning on of the tap, and this would be true, but you could buy many new taps in shops and old ones in junk yards and find that turning them on produced no result at all. The causal explanation reaches much further back. The water is under pressure, in a pipe which connects to the water main, which connects to the water works, where the water is drawn from the reservoir and filtered and tested before being pumped out. I know the reservoir which serves my house: in Summer you can picnic there and watch the waterfowl and buy good ice cream from a van. But what is the causal explanation for the water being in the reservoir?

In asking this question, however, we are getting ahead of ourselves because we have spent no time in thinking about the water delivery system. Take one single element of this: the water main. It is composed of a particular material. Planet earth provided the source of that material; this source was discovered; experiments were done and improvements made; a means of manufacture was devised; machinery was built for the purpose (and the component parts of the machinery had a history of their own); and eventually the lengths of main water pipe were produced, taken to the site, joined and buried under the ground. Other elements of the delivery system have other causal histories. One speaks of a "chain of causality", and it's a useful phrase, but it should not mislead us into seeking the causal explanation of an event in a narrow single strand of simple causes and effects (or effects and causes) reaching backwards in time. Like the pattern in my imaginary carpet, causal explanations are almost infinitely complex and they converge on an event from many directions.

This applies equally to the question of how the water comes to be in the reservoir. How, indeed, does there come to be a reservoir for the water to be in? Its very existence involves the geological history of the planet. And to explain fully the presence of the water would involve a detailed knowledge of rainfall, of climatology, and of the application of this knowledge to this particular site. And sooner or later, if you pursue relentlessly your search for a causal explanation of the water running into your kettle, you will be confronted by the fact that, so far as our present knowledge goes, the earth is one of the very few celestial bodies which has any substantial quantity of water on its surface. So this, too, calls for an explanation. And that explanation takes you all the way back to the origin of the universe, now thought to have occurred some 13.7 billion years ago, and to the ways in which, since the Big Bang, our own planet came to exist and has subsequently developed. This explanation would have to be comprehensive, including for example an explanation of gravity, without which the water would not flow from the tap into the kettle or even stay in the reservoir. And the way in which our planet has developed is linked to the way in which the other component parts of the universe have developed. There really is a sense, isn't there, in which everything seems to be inextricably linked to everything else, in which everything has developed together in mutual inter-dependence?

In practice, no scientist could possibly provide the detailed explanation described in the last paragraph. But we do not doubt that such an explanation could *in principle* be given. The scientists who spend their working lives in seeking to explain aspects of the origin and development of the universe in general, and of the earth in particular, are doing so because causal explanations do exist and are there to be found. Albert Einstein[5] put it in this way:

> To be sure, when the number of factors coming into play in a phenomenological complex is too large, scientific method in most cases fails us .... Nevertheless no one doubts that we are confronted with a causal connection whose causal components are in the

main known to us. Occurrences in this domain are beyond the reach of exact prediction because of the variety of factors in operation, not because of any lack of order in nature.

As Einstein suggests, it is characteristic of causal chains – or of a multiplicity of inter-dependent causal chains – that they run both ways. If, in principle, you could follow them into the past then, in principle, you could have grabbed hold of them at some past time and let them take you into the future. If, for example, you were alive in 1814, you could – again, of course, in principle – have predicted what results causality was going to produce in the course of some later year.

The year of 1814 is chosen because it was in this year that the French physicist, mathematician and philosopher, Pierre Simon Laplace, invented a character who will play a part in this book. Laplace[6] said this:

> We may regard the present state of the universe as the effect of its past and the cause of its future. An intellect which at a certain moment would know all forces that set nature in motion, and all positions of all items of which nature is composed, if this intellect were also vast enough to submit these data to analysis, it would embrace in a single formula the movements of the greatest bodies of the universe and those of the tiniest atom; for such an intellect nothing would be uncertain and the future just like the past would be present before its eyes.

The entity in possession of this omniscient intellect has come to be called "Laplace's Demon". Laplace's Demon is a useful invention. The things which, for humans, can be done only in principle, this hypothetical entity could do in practice. And as a result, says Laplace, his Demon could predict the future.

Some philosophers object to this idea on the ground that the

Demon would need to have an infinite amount of knowledge, and an entity with infinite knowledge is a logical impossibility. (This, on the face of it, is an argument which would seem to dispose rather too easily of God.) But this point need not detain us. Laplace's purpose was only to illuminate the notion of scientific determinism, and the causes relevant to any particular effect must surely be finite anyway.

If we come back for a moment to the kitchen tap, we can already see that a full causal explanation of the water running out of it is not going to be a simple one. And there's one important element in this explanation which we have not even touched on yet. Every aspect of the system which takes the water from the reservoir, purifies it, tests it, and delivers it through pipes to your home, together with the design and manufacture of the kitchen tap itself, is the result of human activity. Human beings created all these things, and without human beings they would not exist. And of course a full causal explanation for the existence of human beings would be every bit as complex as one for the existence of the water in the reservoir (and would include it, because no life can exist without water) and this explanation, too, would take you back to the origin of the universe. And here again the causal chains would stretch forwards and backwards. And if Laplace's Demon were to view the situation at a time when none of the components of the water system had been invented, he would nonetheless have been able to foresee their invention and their use in the system which delivers the water to your kitchen tap.

Or would he? If you want to believe in free will you have to say, "No he wouldn't". The essence of determinism is that the complex causal chains which bring a human being into existence run on so as to create, through the interaction of hereditary characteristics and environmental influences, his or her character, with all its motivations, its desires and constraints, and that they then run on through that

11

character to cause or determine his or her behaviour. But the belief that this is so cannot be reconciled with a belief in free will. Free will demands that the causal chains do not run through us to determine our actions. Our actions are instead the result of something called free will and they cannot be predicted even in principle.

So although Laplace's Demon could have predicted the existence of the water, he could not, according to proponents of free will, have predicted the invention or installation of the water system which delivers it to your tap. If people, having created this system, step back and let it operate by itself, it becomes a wholly deterministic system. If they then intervene to make some adjustment or repair, the results of this intervention are similarly determined but the intervention itself is not. Believers in free will must picture human beings as dodging unpredictably in and out of a deterministic flow which is otherwise predictable.

The Demon's inability to predict human actions would of course be all-embracing. If human beings have free will, he could predict nothing which they are going to do – and since events on our planet are now very much influenced by human activity (often for the worse), this means that Laplace was very wrong and his Demon would be unable to predict anything much at all. Human beings, according to a believer in free will, manage somehow to stand outside the natural laws which govern the rest of the universe and, despite being inextricably a part of it, are somehow exempt from the inter-dependent causal relationships of its other elements. Despite being a product of these things, we have the capacity to detach ourselves from them. Quite at what stage of human evolution this capacity arose – and how it arose – is not clear. Nor is it clear at what stage it arises – and how it arises – in the development of an individual human being. But arise it has, and arise it does, at least according to those who believe in free will. Another brief quotation from Einstein[7] shows that he at least did not believe that this is so:

> Scientific research is based on the idea that everything that takes
> place is determined by the laws of nature, and therefore this holds
> for the action of people.

Before we look more closely at the idea of free will, let us look a
little further into the idea of determinism. One day you might turn
on the kitchen tap and find that nothing happens. It's a bit of a
shock, but it doesn't make you doubt causality: on the contrary, you
feel confident that there's a causal explanation for it somewhere.
Maybe the water main has burst. Maybe the filtration plant has gone
wrong. Maybe the reservoir is empty. And there is an analogy here
with human beings. If our actions are indeed determined, as I
believe, then they are determined, not only by our being the people
we are, but by all the influences, including external ones, which bear
upon us up to the moment when we do or refrain from an act. The
things that determine what you do are still happening to you.

   An example is provided by another character who will appear
several times in this book. Let's call him Burglar Bill. This Burglar
Bill is not meant to resemble, except in his occupation, any fictional
character of the same name[8]. Our Burglar Bill is an habitual burglar.
At this stage of his life, he makes his living by breaking into houses
and other properties after nightfall and stealing what he finds inside.
He has emerged not very long ago from a miserable childhood
which has left him with strong anti-social tendencies. And sadly,
although he has no mental illness which a psychiatrist would
recognise as such, he has a serious drug addiction which he has to
pay for. When we meet him, Burglar Bill has run out of money and
is standing, in the small hours of the morning, in a dark and deserted
road outside a large house which he believes to be currently
unoccupied but by no means devoid of valuables and which looks
quite easy to break into. He has no qualms about burglary: if the
truth be told, he gets rather a kick out of it. So it certainly looks,

from what we know of him, as if Bill is going to break into the house. But if, at the last minute, a policeman should turn the corner and start walking towards him, he is unlikely to do so. An unexpected bit of external causation has been added to the causal factors which already exist within him. Or, to put it another way, one of the factors which already exists within him – namely, the desire not to get caught and suffer a penalty – has been aroused by this external event.

Although the causal factors which go to determine human behaviour, according to a determinist like me, are almost unimaginably complex, the idea of determinism is simplicity itself. Determinism is no more than a natural process of cause and effect which works its way towards our existence, then encompasses our existence and everything we think and feel and do, and then passes on, after our deaths, to other things. But very many people are startled and affronted by the suggestion that their behaviour is determined, and this may be partly because they misunderstand determinism. They may think of it as Fate with a capital F. They may see it as an inexorable and alien force in the face of which they are powerless: one against which they may struggle but, if they do, will struggle in vain.

Somerset Maugham, in his play *Sheppey*, re-tells an old Arabian fable. A merchant in Baghdad has a servant who goes into the market place to buy food. While there, he is jostled by a figure whom he recognises as Death. He returns to his master, terrified, and says that Death made a threatening gesture towards him. He begs the master to lend him his horse so that he may leave Baghdad and ride to Samarra, where he thinks Death will not find him and he will thus avoid his fate. His master lends him the horse, the servant rides off and the master himself then goes to the market place where he sees Death and asks for an explanation of the threatening gesture. Death replies that it was not a threatening gesture at all but rather a start of surprise: "I was astonished to see him in Baghdad, for I had an appointment with him tonight in Samarra."

It is a lovely story, but this idea of fleeing in vain from a remorseless fate, or trying in vain to escape it, has nothing to do with determinism. Determinism works through our wishes and desires, not against them. These wishes and desires are products of the process of cause and effect which is determinism, and they serve in turn to further that process. The popular idea of fate, by contrast, seems to be that of an end not brought about by a causal chain but imposed by some implacable and omnipotent authority. This wrong view has to be exposed and jettisoned before we go any further because otherwise we shall never be able to judge determinism fairly. When I was gathering material for this book I summoned up the courage to approach a writer, well known and with a great intellectual reputation, whose recent book had incidentally espoused the idea of free will. I questioned this, but in his reply he stuck to his guns: he said he would find it difficult to accept, for example, that particular choices he had made in relation to the legacies in his Will (which, it so happened, I had drawn up years ago when I practised as a solicitor) were "in some sense settled for me". Well of course he would, and so would I, but there is really no sense in which determinism requires us to believe this. It is we alone who make our choices, but we make them in the way we do because we are the people we are; and we are the people we are because of the causal factors which have made us that way. There is nothing alarming about this. Wouldn't it be alarming if it were not so?

3.

What is free will?

In the previous chapter I took it for granted that, in human affairs, determinism would preclude free will, and free will would preclude determinism. I believe this to be true, but now I need to retrace my steps and work more carefully towards that conclusion.

Some philosophers – they have come, for obvious reasons, to be known as the compatibilists – have taken the view that determinism and free will are in fact compatible with one another. All that free will requires, according to them, is that people are free to do what they *choose* to do: the fact that their choices are determined, by causality stretching back to a time before their births, does not seem to these philosophers to matter. Provided that people are not physically compelled to act in a particular way, or coerced into doing so by some other external means, and provided that they are not mentally ill, they are free in the only sense in which they can be free – and this freedom may be called free will. To qualify as an exercise of free will, a compatibilist asks only that an act be *voluntary*.

This view is opposed by the incompatibilists, who agree that freedom from compulsion or coercion or illness is indeed the only kind of freedom that can exist if determinism is true, but who are adamant that this does not amount to free will in any meaningful sense. They see the compatibilist position as something of a cop-out. To say that people are (unless compelled, coerced or ill) free to do what they choose to do is really to say nothing of substance unless their *choice* of what to do is also free – and compatibilists don't deny that determinism would rule out this kind of freedom. Laplace's Demon could still make his predictions with complete confidence. To an incompatibilist, the compatibilists are trying to maintain a belief in free will by closing their eyes to the real problem, trying to make the best of a bad job. To the philosopher William James compatibilism was a "quagmire of evasion" and to Immanuel Kant (more of him later) "a wretched subterfuge"[9].

Part of the difficulty here is that the two groups are using the term "free will" in different senses. And in fairness to the compatibilists it has to be admitted that, in everyday life, we do sometimes use the phrase in the sense in which they use it. Suppose that, wishing to lavish a little extra praise on Sarah, a good person who has done a good deed, we emphasise that she did it "of her own free will". Here we are probably using the expression to mean no more than the compatibilists mean by it. All we are saying is that the good deed was not forced upon her in any way: it was done simply because, out of the goodness of her heart, she chose to do it. And we are pointing out, implicitly, that it demonstrates how good her heart is: it shows the kindly nature of her personality and it is really this that we are praising her for. The fact that Sarah's personality is a product of past events over which she herself had no control does not concern us here and is not contradicted by this use of the term "free will".

We need to bear in mind what Humpty Dumpty said "in a rather scornful tone" in *Alice Through the Looking-Glass*: "When I use a word it means just what I choose it to mean – neither more nor less." The meaning of "free will" is certainly not implicit in the phrase itself: if it were, there might be less argument about whether it exists or not. In fact, however, it is not at all clear what the "will" is supposed to be – there is no particular part of the personality which can be labelled in this way – or, still more important, what it is supposed to be free from. Free merely from coercion, as the compatibilists would have it, or free from causality as well?

Something needs to be emphasised at this point. The free will with which this book is concerned is the free will which our society upholds and in which nearly all of its individual members profess to believe. And this *isn't* a compatibilist free will. If determinism is true, then the way I choose to act is determined by the hereditary and environmental forces which have created and shaped me, and the absence of coercion serves only to ensure that nothing stops me from acting in this way. There is no room here for any internal freedom. A computer which is following a programme will continue to do so unless and until a virus interferes with it or you pull the plug on it or hit it with a hammer, yet no one would say that it had free will.

But let us explore the popular conception of free will by means of a practical example. Why not take that of Burglar Bill, who is still standing outside the empty house? From what we know of him it seems clear that, barring the appearance of a policeman or some other external factor, he is going to break in. We don't know quite enough about him to be sure of this. Perhaps he has a girlfriend who has been begging him to give up his life of crime and perhaps, as he stands there, something brings her entreaties to the forefront of his mind, thus introducing another causal factor into the situation, and he yields to them. But let us assume that nothing of this sort occurs and that his desire to break into the house remains wholehearted and unimpaired. Laplace's Demon, if he were present, would predict the break-in, and let us assume that it happens and that Bill walks away with a number of very valuable items. And maybe the house isn't empty at all, but is occupied by a woman and a child who come upon him unexpectedly and are both traumatised by the experience.

We are going to *blame* Burglar Bill, aren't we? We are going to think him *culpable*. The criminal law is going punish him if he should be caught and we are going to think that he *deserves* his punishment. Some of us may even think he is a young thug who deserves a much harsher punishment than he actually receives. It is clear that these views cannot be justified merely on the basis that he is free from coercion. They can be justified, if at all, only on the basis that he is endowed with a kind of free will which would enable him, instead of choosing to break into the house, to choose instead to walk away from it, go home to bed and never offend the law again – and which would mean *that he might actually do this*. These last words are important. The moral *condemnation* which we visit upon Burglar Bill, the belief that he richly *deserves* punishment as a form of *retribution* (we call it "retributory justice"), depend upon there being a genuine possibility that he might actually, in the real world, refrain from breaking into the house. If we want to justify this condemnation, and this belief, we must uphold a kind of free will which would entail this consequence – a free will which would mean that Bill might really and truly turn decisively on his heel and walk away. And that he might do this despite (as we have assumed) having no motivation to do it. It is, in other words, a free will which is free from causality - free from determinism - as well as from coercion. And it is to this free will that I shall refer when I use the phrase from here onwards.

Can we justify belief in such a thing? Can we find any basis for it? No one can sensibly deny that the human personality is formed by a combination of genetic inheritance and environmental influences, but might these very things still serve in some way to build into it a capacity which amounts to the free will we are looking for? Most of those who believe in free will must surely think, if they think about it at all, that this is how it arises.

The idea that a part of the personality amounts to something like an arbitrator – a function which mediates between other parts of the personality – is not in itself outlandish. On Freud's formulation, for example, the mind can be pictured as consisting of id, ego and super-ego (each of them part conscious and part unconscious). The id consists of one's unbridled drives towards selfish emotional satisfaction. The super-ego consists of the prohibitions formed gradually as one grows up – and these are not necessarily to be equated with a "good" conscience because they can develop in such a way as to be weak or perverse on the one hand or tyrannical and harmful on the other. (Freud's paper *Criminals from a Sense of Guilt* [10] suggests that the possessor of a strong but perverse conscience may even be driven to commit crimes in order to obtain punishment.) And the ego approximates most closely to one's individual selfhood and serves as a buffer (or, if you like, a kind of arbitrator) between the other two, enabling its possessor to act in his or her long-term interests. Freud coined the term "ego strength" to describe the ego's ability to do this job, because a weak ego is likely to be overwhelmed by one side or the other.

Now it is certainly true, on this formulation, that a person whose behaviour is mediated by a strong conscious ego may be said to be more "in control of himself" or "in control of herself" than someone of whom this is not true. And it looks as if Burglar Bill has a pretty weak ego and that he might not find himself in his present situation if he had a stronger one. But this is getting us nowhere in our search for free will. Freud himself was a determinist [11] and his idea of the ego was of a part of the personality which develops along with the rest of it, its strength or weakness determined by factors which are ascertainable. There is nothing about Freud's ego which detaches it from causality, nothing about its nature or functioning, in any individual person, which Laplace's Demon would not be able to predict.

No, what we need to find within the mind (or the brain) of a human being, if free will is ever to get to the starting gate, is something which would stop the causality which formed him or her from running on into his or her feelings, thoughts and actions. It must break the causal chain, stopping causality dead in its tracks. It must, in short, amount not merely to an arbitrator but to what philosophers sometimes call an *originator*. Ted Honderich, the determinist philosopher who made a brief appearance in Chapter 1, says[12] that no one has ever begun to answer "the question of the nature of an originator", and this is no surprise because the idea is surely an absurdity. It has been called "a prime mover unmoved". What this seems to mean is that it is a function within the personality which is the cause or origin of our behaviour but is not itself caused by anything at all. Of course one can see the superficial attractions of such a thing: it would be the answer to the prayers of anyone who couldn't find a flaw in the idea of determinism but wanted to go on believing in the idea of free will. But let us look at it more closely.

Some obvious questions present themselves. If it really is uncaused, how does it come to exist? Don't ask. If it springs up spontaneously, self-generating, coming from nowhere, how is it connected with the person who has it? Don't ask. If we are all proud possessors of an originator, why don't we all behave in the same way – or is my originator a better or worse originator than your originator and, if so, how are you and I responsible for that? Again, don't ask.

No, but seriously: one thing which must be true of an originator, if it is to be a foundation for free will, is that it is under the control of the person who possesses it. If that were not so, then the good deed which Sarah did could not reflect credit on her, and the crime which Burglar Bill committed could not reflect discredit on him, because in each case it would be the originator (not Sarah, not Bill) that did it. No, the originator must be something which a person wields, employs or makes use of. And why would a person make use of an originator except to attain some end which he or she wants to attain? But the originator cannot be conceived of as a means to the ends dictated by the person's wishes, because then the chain of causation would run straight through the originator and it could not be the origin of anything. So are we supposed to picture it as some sort of mystical force which interposes itself between a person's motivation to do some act and the doing of the act itself, somehow severing the causal connection between the two (perhaps even frustrating the act altogether) while at the same time being under the person's control? No one in their right mind could believe in such a thing.

Look. If someone acts in a particular way, can we legitimately ask *why* they did so? Does it make *sense* to ask why? Is this a question which is meaningful and could in principle be answered even if, barring such scientific developments as we cannot even begin to imagine, it can never be answered in full detail? If it is, then there is simply no room for free will. We have assumed that Burglar Bill has a single-minded desire to break into the house. Yet an adherent of free will would still maintain that he might, by means of this faculty, refrain from doing so. How would he manage it? By using his free will somehow to inflate or increase the plainly inadequate power of any conscience he may have? How could he do this and, more to the point, *why* would he do it? Certainly not because he has a strong conscience; so *why*? There can be no answer. The price you have to pay for believing in an originator – the price you pay for believing in free will – is that you cannot know why anyone does anything. You can never ask why free will was exercised in this way rather than that way, because to do so would be to presuppose that its exercise had a causal explanation, and you cannot admit causality because causality is determinism. Laplace's Demon would be able to foresee it and the whole house of cards would collapse.

If someone habitually does bad things, as perhaps Burglar Bill does, we think that this sheds light on their character; and if someone like Sarah consistently does good things, we think the same. But this is so only if the things done are *determined* by the person's character. If we cannot say that they are, because we have to say instead that they are an expression of a free will which does not depend upon character – and this *is* what we have to say if we believe that Bill might turn away and go home – then we have to accept that deeds do *not* shed light on character. Bill may have a good character but still behave badly, and if he has a bad character he may still start behaving like a saint; and Sarah, despite all her good deeds, may have a character as black as ink.

Can we now try to answer the question which heads this chapter by formulating a definition of free will – of the kind of free will in which we must believe if we want to believe that Burglar Bill might actually refrain from what he does and so is to blame for doing it? Can we perhaps say that it is something – a capacity, a faculty, a facility? – possession of which entails the consequence that its possessor is able to act against his or her own wishes and may actually do so? Do you find that a definition of something you really can believe in? Me neither. It is not so much a nonsensical definition as a definition of something which is nonsensical.

But free will, or a belief in what we call free will, is woven deeply into our culture and there is more to be said about it. Is there really no way in which it can be substantiated? Let us try to find one.

PART II

CAN WE RESCUE FREE WILL?

4.

Could he have done otherwise?

What rejoinder might a proponent of free will want to make to the last chapter? Perhaps one like this: "Oh, come off it! Are you saying – are you really saying – that Burglar Bill *had* to break in, couldn't have *helped* breaking in, couldn't have done *otherwise* than to break in?" Many people, some philosophers among them, have certainly taken a very simple view about free will. They presuppose that someone has done some particular act and then they ask the question which heads this chapter. They tend to think that the reply must be, "Yes, of course he could", and that this reply is all that's needed to demonstrate the existence of free will.

But there is something concealed in the question which destroys the significance of this reply. If Fred goes out in his best suit without protection against the weather, gets caught in a downpour and returns home soaked to the skin, some helpful bystander might say, "You could have taken your umbrella, couldn't you?" Fred might reply politely (because he is not easily provoked), "Yes I could. It is in the umbrella stand near the front door and I could easily have taken it if I had wanted to, but I didn't want to because I find it a bit of an encumbrance and I thought (wrongly as it turned out) that the weather would hold."

The trouble with the question, "Could he have done otherwise?", is that it ignores human motivation. Before you can answer it in any particular case, you have to imagine or suppose an attempt to do otherwise fuelled by a *wish* to do otherwise, and then you have to decide whether or not the attempt would be successful. And of course it's perfectly true that it would always be successful (unless it were prevented by some outside circumstance) because determinism acts through our wishes, not against them. If Fred had wished to take his umbrella he could and would have done so. But unless the wish exists, the attempt will not be made and the other course of action will certainly not be taken. And the fact that the wish doesn't exist is inherent in the question because (assuming no coercion) the act which the person actually did, and not some other act, must have been the act he wished to do. But are you perhaps still inclined to doubt that the word "could" presupposes a wish? If so, imagine that I re-phrased the question and asked, "Could he have done otherwise if he didn't want to?" The only answer to *this* is, "What sort of a question is that?" The wish which was implied in the original question has now been subtracted from it and the result is a nonsense. If the answer, "Yes", to "Could he have done otherwise?", seems to contradict determinism, this is only because the determining factors have been excluded from the question.

So the only possible answer to, "Could he have done otherwise?", is, "Yes, if he had chosen to do otherwise." And this answer has a familiar ring, doesn't it? We have come full circle and found ourselves back with the compatibilists at the start of the last chapter.

Poor old Burglar Bill is still standing outside the house. He is in reasonably good health, his mobility unimpaired (as indeed it would have to be if he were to break in), so he would be physically capable of turning his back on the house and walking away. But if we take this to mean that he has free will, we are simply joining forces with the compatibilists. We agree with them in saying that Bill is free to implement any choice he may make, so if he chose to break in he would be able to do so, and if he chose not to break in he would be able to go home to bed (assuming always that he has a home and a bed). But as we have already noticed, none of this adds up to free will in the incompatibilist sense - free will of the kind in which we must believe if we want to think that Bill might really turn away - because it leaves untouched the question of whether his *choice* is free, as distinct from being determined by the motivation within his personality. There would be nothing to stop Burglar Bill from turning away if he had the wish to do so; but he didn't have that wish. His history – his genetic inheritance and the influences of his past life – have not endowed him with it. And since he didn't wish to turn away, there was no actual possibility that he would.

When we have within ourselves the motivation to do something, we do that thing; and when we have no motivation to do something, we do not do it. But if, contrary to his expectations, the police catch Bill after the burglary, he would be unwise to make this point. He will do himself no good at all if he stands up in court and says that he broke into the house because he had a wholehearted desire to do so and no wish whatever to refrain from doing so. This, in the eyes of our society, is no excuse: paradoxically, it may serve only to increase our outrage and condemnation.

If you are looking for a simple test for the existence of real free will, then the question to ask, surely, is not, "Could he have done otherwise?", but rather, "*Might* he have done otherwise?" In other words, given all the circumstances, and given the personality or the character which he had when he did the act in question, might he nonetheless, in the real world, actually have refrained from doing it and done something else? This is a very different question because it takes account of his motivations, and the answer to it is not, "Yes, of course", but, " No, of course not".

Consider finally the possibility of two Burglar Bills. Perhaps they are standing in different but identical streets outside different but identical houses, or perhaps, if you are very imaginative, you can picture them standing outside the same house in parallel universes. Either way the point about these two Bills is that they are exactly the same – identical in personality down to the minutest detail – and there is no difference in the external factors which might influence their behaviour. In all these circumstances, do you think one of them might break into the house and the other might go home to bed? If you don't, you are a determinist.

5.

What about conscience?

Burglar Bill has been portrayed as having no moral inhibitions whatever about breaking into the house: his wish to do so is wholehearted and that's why he does it. Is this plausible? Can it really be that he has no conscience? Doesn't everyone have a conscience? And doesn't Burglar Bill behave in this way because he somehow chooses to ignore his?

My dictionary defines conscience as "a moral sense of right and wrong". Bill knows that society in general (though perhaps not the company which he himself keeps) thinks it wrong to break into people's houses and wrong to steal, but this knowledge in itself will not necessarily make him disinclined to do these things. A test of criminal responsibility is the ability to "tell right from wrong", and this plays a part in deciding upon the age of criminal responsibility (set in this country at 10 years, very nearly the lowest in Europe), but the knowledge that an act is "wrong" does not necessarily carry with it any motivation to abstain from the act. Bill knows also that, because society takes this view and expresses it through the criminal law, he will be punished if he gets caught, but that has nothing to do with conscience – and in any case he doesn't believe that he will be caught. What Bill needs if he is to be *motivated* to refrain from wrongful acts is the "moral sense" to which the dictionary refers. Unless he feels within himself a prohibition, an inhibition, a constraint - something, in other words, which would make him feel guilty, ashamed or remorseful if he went against it - his behaviour will not be influenced for the better. And we have assumed that, at least so far as burglary is concerned, he doesn't have anything like this.

The idea that "everyone has a conscience" is a myth put about by people who do have consciences and project the sort of consciences they have on to everyone else. In reality, the development of a good conscience, involving as it does the capacity for empathy with other people, requires good parenting – parenting which includes loving and supportive guidance. And in reality there are many people like Bill who, mainly because of their upbringing, don't have anything much in the way of a conscience at all and certainly don't have one which law abiding citizens would call "normal". The conscience is something which develops, well or badly, within the individual, like any other part of the personality. It is in any case a very elusive concept. It isn't a single entity but a loose collection of motivations and prohibitions which incline people to behave in ways which are thought, for the time being, to be socially desirable. Times change, of course, and acts dictated by the conscience of one generation, or by that of one society, may seem cruel or destructive to another. Someone brought up in a tribe of head-hunters might well have felt pangs of conscience if he had failed to join his fellows in a head-hunting expedition.

It's true that motivations are seldom quite as uncomplicated as those with which Burglar Bill has been credited. In practice we live our lives by charting a course through a certain amount of discordance within ourselves, weaker desires being overcome by stronger ones. Many of us get up in the morning only because our wish, or sense of obligation, to do things during the day is stronger than our wish to stay in bed. People are impelled to act, most of the time, not by a single motivation but by what could be called a preponderance of motivation. Perhaps Bill was not quite as single-minded as we have supposed. Perhaps he had some residual conscientious wish to kick his drug habit, kick his burgling habit, and live a better life, but if so this wish was too weak to prevail over contrary impulses and it was this relative weakness that determined his decision to break in.

When Saint Paul in his *Epistle to the Romans* (7:19) said, "For the good that I would I do not: but the evil that I would not, that I do", he spoke for many of us. What he was complaining about was a conflict of motivation within himself. Undoubtedly he had a conscience, and almost certainly a strong one, but although this made him wish to do good things and not to do bad ones, these wishes were not always stronger than the contrary desires (conscious or otherwise) to which he was subject. As a result, according to him, he sometimes did bad things. And of course I would assert that this result was determined: it is certainly true that the free will which he must have thought he had did not enable him to avoid it.

From what we know of Saint Paul, it seems unlikely that, if he had been reincarnated in the last century and gone to the cinema, he would have felt any urge to join in the chorus of Marlene Dietrich's song in *The Blue Angel*:

> Fallin' in love again
> Never wanted to
> What am I to do?
> Can't help it.

But the Dietrich character's complaint is nonetheless the same as his, and her claim that she "never wanted to" echoes his own disavowal of any wish to do evil. Yet if both were sincere in this disavowal, both must nonetheless have had within themselves a strong unacknowledged desire to do what they didn't consciously wish to do. As Marlene Dietrich's character explains later in the song, "Play it how I may, I was made that way".

Samuel Butler's novel *Erewhon* was first published in 1872. Its protagonist crossed a mountain range and came upon an undiscovered country – undiscovered, that is, like north America when Columbus discovered it, except by the people who actually lived there. Discovery was not good news for native Americans, but the people of Erewhon were not disadvantaged because they had only this single visitor. When he explored the attitudes and customs of these people, however, he found them strange indeed. For example, illness was regarded as immoral - a crime to be punished - whereas what we would call crime was treated as an illness deserving of sympathy, even if the sympathy is sometimes a little muted [13]:

> The fact … that the Erewhonians attach none of that guilt to crime which they do to physical ailments, does not prevent the more selfish among them from neglecting a friend who has robbed a bank, for instance, till he has fully recovered; but it does prevent them from even thinking of treating criminals with that contemptuous tone which would seem to say, "I, if I were you, should be a better man than you are".

In reading *Erewhon*, one is never quite sure how far Butler's tongue is in his cheek, but in the last bit of this quotation I suspect his cheek is empty. In our civilisation now this really *is* the attitude which we bring to bear on criminals. Let this thought - *if I were you, I should be a better man than you are* - marinate for a few moments. If we analyse it soberly, we can see that it's crazy. But we don't analyse it. We don't even express it in words. Yet we harbour it nonetheless: in fact, we harbour it all the more. If I were you, of *course* I shouldn't be better than you: I should be just the same as you, and I should behave just as you do. And if readers of this book were to carry away with them only one single thought, I should like that to be it.

34

6.

What about choice?

In 1957 a biography of Bertrand Russell (mathematician, philosopher, social reformer, writer and, to me and to very many, a genuinely awesome and charismatic figure) was published: *Bertrand Russell: The Passionate Sceptic* by Alan Wood [14]. It proved to be a bit premature – Russell did not die until 1970 – and no doubt it had its shortcomings, but I thought the title was good and, at the time, I loved the book. Wood records that he had arguments with Russell on the subject of free will and determinism. Wood pointed proudly to his having given up smoking as "a plain example of free will". Russell, with a patience you have to admire, replied, "I do not deny your moral pride, but I deny you have any occasion for it." Wood adds sadly that, "as in most discussions on this subject, we never got much further".

Wood doesn't seem to have given any deep thought to the problem: for him (if I may hark back to my first chapter) the penny had certainly not dropped. Just because of that, his example of free will is interesting: it is exactly the sort of example which many people would give. Here, after all, is someone who has an established smoking habit and suddenly chooses to break it and manages successfully to do so. If this isn't an example of free will, he'd like to know what is. But he didn't give up smoking for no reason: probably he gave it up because he realised it was bad for his health. Perhaps his doctor or his wife, or both, had urged him to give it up. There must, mustn't there, have been a causal explanation for what he did, and this must lie in the way in which his mind, itself the product of genetic inheritance and past influences, processed and reacted to new causal factors consisting in information or exhortations? Can Alan Wood really have supposed that determinism would have condemned him to go on smoking for ever? Perhaps Russell made some of these points to him; if so, he would have put them better than I have.

Nonetheless, it is choice – the experience of choosing between alternatives – that, for very many people, constitutes both the essence and the proof of free will. "I know I have a *choice*", they will say and that, for them, is the end of the matter. And it is true, of course, that we do make choices every hour, perhaps every minute, of our lives. Some choices are so easy that they hardly seem like choices at all: from what we know of Burglar Bill, his choice between breaking in and walking away falls into this category. But some choices present us with a real dilemma. Let me introduce Tom, who had a choice like this. There seemed to be difficulties for every solution, cons as well as pros for every possible course of action. The problem seemed almost insoluble and he spent a long time agonising over it, returning to it again and again, still failing to see any clear way forward. He knew he had to make a choice and, in the end, he did. Can it really be true that this choice was determined from the start? Surely, surely, all that agonising must have been evidence of free will?

But must it? It is certainly evidence that the real life situation was a difficult one and that there were, within Tom's personality, forces, desires, restraints and prohibitions which were evenly balanced, difficult to reconcile. And it must be true that a function of consciousness is to allow possible courses of action to be reviewed and evaluated with foresight, and that this can sometimes be a hard and prolonged process. (I don't understand what consciousness really *is*, any more than anyone else does, but I do see this as being one of its functions and I can see why, if once a glimmer of it appeared in our remote ancestors, evolution favoured its development.) But the crucial question, surely, is whether, when the choice is eventually made, Tom felt that it was made for a reason or reasons. If so, then it was not undetermined; and isn't it perfectly possible that Laplace's Demon could have anticipated the twists and turns which preceded it? These twists and turns, far from being a pointless and superfluous preliminary to a conclusion which in some sense already existed, were themselves an essential part of the determining process: the decision couldn't have been reached without them and, if it had been, would have been meaningless and unsatisfactory to the person who reached it.

It should be emphasised, of course, that the real *causes* of a person's choice are not necessarily to be equated with the reasons for which he or she thinks it is made. To begin with, many of our motivations are built so deeply into our personalities that they are never acknowledged at all (think of Saint Paul, think of the Marlene Dietrich character): the existence of unconscious mental processes is widely recognised today – they are said to dwarf our consciousness – and so is the fact that the reasons which we give, to ourselves or to others, for taking a decision may be no more than rationalisations. And even if we leave these things aside it would still be true that no one could be fully aware of all the causal factors involved in the making of a choice.

But the point to be emphasised is that there is really nothing about the experience of choosing which makes it seem like an experience of free will. In making the decision, we do not feel that we can, or do, divorce ourselves from the desires and prohibitions which already exist within us: on the contrary our aim is to make a decision which, so far as possible, reconciles and gives expression to them. As we review the options, we strive to make what seems to us the "right" choice, but the right choice is the choice which conforms most closely to the preponderance of our own conscious or unconscious motivations. And although we know that we could have chosen differently if we had had the motivation to do so, we know also that we didn't have that motivation. The experience of choosing is an experience of determinism which would be recognisable as such if we were willing to recognise it.

There is of course a real difference between the experience of making a conscious decision, perhaps preceded by a lot of thought, and the experience of being overwhelmed by strong emotions which seem to bypass all thought. Occasionally, for some of us, the "red mist" descends and we do some violent act which, when we "come to", we can hardly remember because we "don't know what came over" us. The absence of free will from this second experience is pretty obvious: some legal jurisdictions admit "irresistible impulse" as a defence to a criminal charge, and in the United Kingdom the law allows "loss of self-control" as a partial defence to a charge of murder (only partial, mind you, and not to any other crime). But it would be wrong, just because this second kind of experience is so different from the first – from the experience of making a conscious and deliberate choice – to suppose that the difference *consists* in an absence of free will. In truth, free will is absent equally from both kinds of experience because both are the manifestations of a personality – if perhaps of different "parts" of a personality – which has been acquired by a process of cause and effect.

There is a question to be asked about those – Alan Wood among them – who say that the mere experience of choosing convinces them that they have free will. The question is: "How do they suppose their experience would differ from the one they have if the choice *were* determined?" Do they think one of the alternatives wouldn't appear to them at all; or do they think that they would see, in their mind's eye, one of them with a neon sign flashing above it saying, "Choose this one"? Or do they think that they would experience the choice as if it were in some way forced upon them? If so, they misunderstand determinism. Determinists sometimes speak of "the illusion of free will", but this is a very odd sort of illusion. If you see a mirage in the desert, the illusion is of something which conforms with the laws of nature and might really be there. But the illusion of free will, surely, is an illusion of something incomprehensible: an illusion of an illusion?

Determinist philosophers still hold to their views despite their subjective experience of choosing, while philosophers who seek to uphold free will do not suggest that this experience is of itself conclusive in their favour. The issue here is not whether we make choices (of course we do) but whether the choices we make have causal explanations and, if so, whether those explanations lie within ourselves - in our being the people we are, and in the factors which have made us that way. If they do, that's determinism. If they don't, then surely that's pretty alarming.

7.

What about religion?

The involvement of the Christian religion in the debate about free will and determinism makes a strange story. On the face of it, the religious position seems clear enough. The concept of "sin" is central to Christianity: to put it bluntly and simply, a life of sin sets you on course for hell, and one of virtue sets you on course for heaven. Such beliefs may well have an effect upon believers which does not depend upon the existence of free will: determinists would not deny that, in common with other causal factors within the personality, they may play a part in improving people's behaviour. But the punishment of sin and the reward of virtue in the afterlife are seen by the religious as being essentially *deserved* and this *does* depend upon free will. It comes as no surprise, therefore, that God is said to have endowed human beings with what is sometimes called "the precious gift of free will".

This God-given free will is pressed into service not only as a justification for eternal damnation or eternal joy, but as an explanation for the terrible suffering which God allows to exist in his world. If God, instead of directing the course of our lives, has given us free will, so allowing us to decide for ourselves how we live them, then of course we have only ourselves to blame for the resulting mess. Or so the argument runs. There is still a great deal of suffering which this explanation seems not to cover - such as that resulting from natural disasters - but perhaps not so much as one might think. American evangelists have explained the Indonesian tsunami in

40

2004 as God's punishment for sexual immorality in tourist nightclubs, the flooding in New Orleans in 2005 as God's judgement on a sinful city and the earthquake in Haiti in 2010 as the result of a "pact with the devil" which Haitians had apparently made over 200 years before. All these things involved a vast amount of death and suffering inflicted on men, women and children who had nothing whatever to do with the sins supposed to have precipitated them. To anyone who does not espouse this primitive brand of religion, such claims must surely seem to portray a God who is as incompetent as he is vindictive.

Be that as it may, we must face up to the assertion that God has given us free will. In this book we are trying to decide whether the idea of free will makes any sense, or whether it is, on the contrary, a logically impossible concept; and this particular assertion is of no help to us in that quest. It is true that, to a believer, God is omnipotent and can perform miracles, so perhaps there is some sense in which he could give us free will even if, like a squared circle, it was to our (God-given) minds an impossibility. But if, in the end, we do conclude that free will really is a nonsense, we would have to conclude also that God had put us in a very strange and awkward position by giving it to us. There seems no way to pursue this point any further.

Paradoxically, however, religion has also made a contribution to this debate from exactly the opposite direction. To very many people, and in a number of different ways, the existence of God has been thought of itself to entail determinism and to rule out the possibility of free will. This is not the place (and I should not have the competence) to attempt a summary of the convoluted history of this thinking. Relying on supposed scriptural authority, Calvin and others preached predestination, asserting that those of us who fall into the category of the damned, and those who fall into the category of the saved – those going either to hell or to heaven – are determined by God before we are born: free will is either non-existent or ineffective. Another group of thinkers has simply found difficulty in reconciling the idea of free will with the idea of God's omniscience. If God has knowledge of everything, including foreknowledge of the future, so that the course of our own lives is known to God before they begin, does this not mean that the course of our lives is determined? Would it not be impossible for our lives to deviate in any way from the course God knows they are going to take, with the result that free will cannot exist?

Arguments about this have ebbed and flowed at least since the time of St. Augustine of Hippo (354–430). Having regard to the theme of this book, it would be tempting to espouse the views of those who think that God's omniscience entails determinism, but that would be dishonest. If free will were a possibility then surely God's foreknowledge of all our future conduct would not preclude it, because God is not to be equated with Laplace's Demon. If all our future conduct were known to Laplace's Demon, that would indeed rule out the possibility of free will; but this is because the Demon can forecast the future only by applying his unlimited intelligence and knowledge to the operation of causality and natural laws. Free will would break into this process, disrupt it and upset all his calculations, because his hypothetical knowledge is scientific, not miraculous. God's knowledge, on the other hand, *is* miraculous; and although it might take a two-fold miracle for God both to grant us free will and to know how we would exercise it, miracles are, after all, his *forte*.

If you think free will has come into existence by miraculous means, it would probably be impossible to convince you otherwise. If, on the other hand, you side with the Calvinists, or with those who simply think that God's omniscience precludes free will, it would probably be impossible to convince you that, although you might have reached the right conclusion, you would have done so by the wrong road. But perhaps it is appropriate nonetheless to make one final comment. In this country, our state is a secular state, and if the only possible justification for free will were to be found in religious doctrine, then it would surely be wrong to let the idea play a part in our institutions.

8.

What about chance?

Voltaire [15] thought that there was no such thing as pure chance. "Chance is a word devoid of sense," he said; "nothing can exist without a cause." But do modern scientific developments prove him wrong? If so, does this serve to dethrone Laplace's Demon, to invalidate his deterministic view of the world, and perhaps even to provide a foothold for free will?

Judged according to the scientific knowledge of his time, Voltaire was surely right. The things we are accustomed to speak of as happening by "chance" are not uncaused: they are still links in a deterministic chain. To speak of a "chance meeting", for example, is not to suggest that the meeting was uncaused, but merely that it was unplanned. Called upon to give the best example of "chance" that they can think of, most people would probably come up with the outcome of throwing dice or spinning a coin. And for all practical purposes, this *is* chance because no human being could forecast it. But Laplace's Demon could, because if the exact force and angle of the spin or throw is known, together with every last detail of the conditions prevailing at the time, the outcome is predictable in principle. Tom, the character in Chapter 6 who wrestled for so long with an almost impossible choice, might in the end have tired of the struggle and made the decision by flipping a coin; but the Demon would have been able to forecast both his decision to do so and the result of the flipping. Determinism still rules.

And it is a matter of everyday experience that determinism can produce results which seem to be undetermined. After a night in the garage, my car's engine would start but often it had no energy: it faltered, stalled and wouldn't move the car. On some days, however, it worked perfectly well. On some days the problem lasted only a few moments, on others for five minutes. On some days a warning sign came up saying here was something wrong with the alternator, on other days it didn't. And although an environmental factor – the cold – seemed usually to make matters worse, this wasn't always so. Yet quite clearly this oddly inconsistent behaviour was not uncaused. Another example might be the behaviour of the computer on which this book is being constructed. It seems to react in different ways at different times to exactly the same commands, and I sometimes joke feebly that the only place where free will really exists is in my computer. But of course this behaviour is determined, it certainly can't be ascribed to free will, and if I understood more about computers I might not find it inexplicable.

No, in order to oust determinism we should have to find something which is wholly indeterminate, some event which is absolutely and inherently unpredictable, not just in practice but in principle. Has science discovered anything of this kind?

Scientific discoveries have certainly shown that Laplace's Demon, in making his predictions, would have a very much harder time of it than Laplace himself would have supposed. What about chaos theory, for example? Systems which evolve over time are now known to be extremely sensitive to the initial conditions. Hence the so-called "butterfly effect": the fact that something so slight as the beating wings of a butterfly might serve in the course of time to affect the onset of a tornado in another part of the world. (Am I alone in thinking this quite unsurprising?) But there's no suggestion that the end result of this process is anything but determined – the "chaos" in chaos theory is sometimes referred to as "deterministic chaos" – and Laplace's Demon would be able to predict the outcome even though, in the present state of their knowledge, scientists cannot. Then again, what about the random genetic mutations on which the whole of evolution depends? If there were no random mutations there could be no natural selection and we certainly shouldn't be here now because neither the human nor any other species would exist. But does the randomness of random mutations really amount to complete indeterminacy? Evidently not: there are causal explanations for it.

So is there still nothing to dent our faith in determinism – in the predictive ability of the Demon? Well, perhaps something of this kind does exist in the shape of quantum mechanics: the disconcerting behaviour of sub-atomic particles [16]. According to the Copenhagen interpretation, which became an orthodoxy and of which Niels Bohr was the father, these do not exist anywhere until they are observed (though observation seems to show that they can be in two places at once) and, according to Heisenberg's uncertainty principle (which he preferred to call the indeterminacy principle), it is inherently impossible to know both their momentum and their position. At best, quantum physicists deal only in probabilities. The Copenhagen interpretation has other features equally baffling, and Erwin Schrodinger sought to show its incomprehensibility through the thought experiment which has come to be known as Schrodinger's Cat. A cat is confined in a box containing a mechanism which will kill the cat if it is triggered by an unpredictable sub-atomic event that may or may not occur within an hour. When the hour is up, however, the cat is neither alive nor dead until someone actually looks inside the box: it is apparently this act of observation which decides its fate. The American Nobel laureate Richard Feynman, speaking of the Copenhagen interpretation, warned his fellow physicists not to keep asking themselves how it can be like that: "Nobody knows how it can be like that".

Quantum mechanics applies only to the microscopic world, the world of sub-atomic particles. The laws which govern the rest of the universe, the macroscopic world, the world of everyday, are entirely deterministic: first formulated by Newton, these classical laws leave no room for chance. Even when Einstein remodelled them through his Special Theory and General Theory of Relativity, this remained true. And it was largely because of this that Einstein could never accept the indeterminacy which seemed to be inherent in the behaviour of the microscopic world. He famously said on more than one occasion that God (to whom he referred as "the old one") "does not play dice". This remark is open to misunderstanding because the throwing of dice is not really an example of indeterminacy, as we've noticed, and it seems that Einstein had no belief in a personal God anyway, but everyone knew what he meant. Or they thought they did: it may be that Einstein's objection to the Copenhagen interpretation was rather less to its portrayal of the microscopic world as indeterminate than to its portrayal of that world as having no objective reality. Niels Bohr said, "There is no quantum world. There is only an abstract quantum mechanical description. It is wrong to think that the task of physics is to find out how nature is." Einstein disagreed with that; and it seems that Einstein's view has gained a little more ground among physicists since his death.

Fascinating as the oddity of the microscopic world may be, it is of concern to us only in the context of our search for free will. And it is relevant to that search only because it has been suggested that the indeterminacy of the microscopic world provides a basis for free will's existence. So could it be that modern science has at last provided the justification for our centuries-old belief in free will? The answer must be an unequivocal, "No". The dichotomy inherent in the Copenhagen interpretation between the microscopic and the macroscopic worlds was made more perplexing by the fact that no one knew exactly where one ended and the other began, but no one doubted that they were distinct worlds governed by different rules, and no one has doubted that we ourselves live, not in the microscopic world, but in the macroscopic. Even if the microscopic world really is indeterminate, even if it really does lack objective reality, these characteristics do not spill over into our everyday macroscopic world and make that world indeterminate or unreal. The fact that your tea cup is composed of molecules which are composed of atoms which comprise particles which behave unpredictably does not mean that the tea cup itself may jump out of your hands and fly across the room or vanish altogether.

But just suppose for a moment that this is wrong and that the random behaviour of sub-atomic particles could affect human behaviour – that the indeterminacy of the microscopic world really does affect the working of our brains and thus (to some extent at least) the way we behave. Why would that form a basis for free will? It might form a basis for indeterminate, random, capricious, chance behaviour, but not for freely willed behaviour. This is a point of crucial importance. There is an unthinking belief that if only some flaw can be found in the view that human behaviour has a causal explanation, so that there is, as it were, a gap in determinism, free will is bound to rush in to fill the gap as air rushes in to fill a vacuum. The suggestion that the Copenhagen interpretation of the quantum world may form a basis for free will is a striking example of this. Because the idea of free will is so much a part of the atmosphere we breathe, few of its proponents feel the need to address any basic questions about it: what is it, does it make sense, how could it work? They think they know the answers to these questions, or that they don't need to consider them. But behaviour which is the result of chance cannot be ascribed to free will, any more than behaviour which results from determinism.

So there is really no need for opponents of free will to demonstrate that quantum theory is not relevant to human behaviour, because their case would be just as strong if it were. Suppose that people's acts really were the result, not of complete determinism, but rather of a combination of determinism and pure chance. Suppose, in other words, that some links in a causal chain which leads to those acts were replaced by random events which could not be predicted even in principle – that they were beyond the capacity even of Laplace's Demon to foresee. This would not bring us a step closer to free will.

9.

What about mind, brain and consciousness?

In the early 1980s, Benjamin Libet, a neuroscientist, devised and carried out an experiment [17] which seemed to show that the human brain readies itself for an act some 350 milliseconds before we are aware of deciding to do the act. A group of student volunteers were fitted with EEG sensors to pick up signals from the relevant part of the brain, and were asked to give a simple flick of their wrists whenever they felt like doing so. They were told also to watch a large "clock" with a dot which revolved around its face in such a way that the time could be pinpointed with great accuracy, and to note the precise moment at which they decided to carry out the flicking motions. The results showed that their brains gave off a wave of activity, known as the readiness potential, about 350 milliseconds before they made their conscious decision to flick their wrists.

The experiment, which was subsequently repeated many times with similar results, caused consternation, not least to Libet himself. Like everyone else, he had expected to find that the results came out the other way round, so that it was the conscious decision which preceded the brain activity. Instead it looked very much as if our voluntary actions were initiated by unconscious brain processes and not by any conscious decisions of ours. The consternation arose because – and this is the important point – these results were thought to negate free will. Libet said that it might still be possible, before the 350 milliseconds passed, consciously to cancel the flick, so preserving some semblance of free will, although another neuroscientist pointed out that even if this were so it would amount not so much to free will as to "free won't".

Several attempts have been made to suggest that Libet's and similar experiments did not really show what they seemed to show, but more recent experiments tend to confirm their validity. The fact that, by stimulating certain areas of the brain, bodily movements can be produced, is now a commonplace. More interesting are the results of another experiment which showed that a mild electrical stimulation of different parts of the brain caused the subject to feel a conscious "urge" to make movements and that an increase in the current caused the movements actually to take place. The conclusion was drawn that our conscious intentions are no more than by-products of a process which is already taking place unconsciously within our brains. A few moments of honest self-reflection may serve to confirm this. We seldom set out consciously to think the thoughts we think or to feel the feelings we feel. They just pop into our heads - or, more accurately, into our conscious minds - seemingly out of the blue but actually out of the unconscious part of our brains. We do not summon them and quite often we do not welcome them.

Other experiments show that, if a subject is given an arbitrary choice of two buttons to press, and placed within a functional resonance imaging scanner (fMRI), the scanner detects brain patterns which enable experimenters to predict with almost complete accuracy which of the two buttons will be pressed next – and to do so a full six seconds before the subject makes a conscious decision to press that button [18]. As a result of all this, most neuroscientists think that free will does not exist.

These results confront us with the mind-brain problem, the problem of how mind and brain co-exist and how they stand in relation to one another. No solution to this problem has yet gained general acceptance. The philosopher Colin McGinn has suggested [19] that human beings are simply not equipped to solve it: just as a dog couldn't solve the problems about time and space which Einstein solved, so perhaps human beings are intrinsically unable to understand how mind and matter fit together. (This was not an idea which went down well with all of McGinn's fellow philosophers.) Certain things are clear, however. The behaviour of Dr. Strangelove's arm [20], which gave the Nazi salute and tried to strangle him, and which he struggled to bring under control by gripping it in the hand of his other arm, was not altogether far-fetched: "alien hand syndrome" is a recognised neurological condition, caused by physical damage to the brain. In the 19th century a metal pole went clean through the head of a US railway worker, Phineas Gage, and changed him from a hard-working, good-natured character into a bad-tempered, raving and unpleasant one. And a brain tumour has been known to change a man's normal sexual desires into those of a paedophile. It is obvious, in these and very many other ways, that the mind does not exist separately from the brain but is in some sense a product of it. Consciousness certainly doesn't rule OK.

It seems equally clear, on the other hand, that consciousness has some job to do. The simple decisions to act made by the subjects of the experiments described above may have been initiated by their brains, but it is hard to see how the experimenters' instructions could have been conveyed to them (and understood and accepted) except through their conscious minds. And what about the character Tom in Chapter 6 who agonised for a long time over a difficult choice? It is hard to believe that no purpose was served by all the conscious thought which he gave to the issues involved. It may in any case be too simple to draw a distinction between the conscious mind on the one hand and the unconscious brain on the other. The fact that our acts and thoughts are to some extent the result of motivations which are not conscious does not of itself depend in any way on an acceptance of Freud's psychoanalytic theory about the nature of the unconscious mind, but one of the main aims of psychoanalysis is to bring some of these unconscious motives to consciousness, so giving the patient more conscious control over them and, even if questions may hang over the rationale of this process, it would take a brave observer to deny that it has some effect on the patient's behaviour.

The consensus of opinion among neuroscientists that free will is an illusion must be welcome to the author of a book designed to show exactly that, and it would be churlish to look this gift horse in the mouth; but strong doubts must nonetheless be expressed about the twin assumptions which seem to underlie their experiments: that, on the one hand, it is the initiation of an act by unconscious brain processes which *prevents* it from being a product of free will and, on the other, that its initiation by the conscious mind would *make* it a product of free will.

Let's address first the first assumption. The definition of free will which forced itself upon us at the end of Chapter 3 was, I suggested, a definition of something nonsensical. Since then we have been examining ways in which a possible rescue attempt might be mounted but, as you may have guessed, I don't think we are going to find one. However, if free will *could* otherwise exist, would it really be ruled out by the fact that our actions are initiated by the brain rather than by the mind? It doesn't seem quite self-evident that a free will exercised unconsciously by the brain is any *more* nonsensical than a free will exercised consciously by the mind. It's true of course that the brain, as a lump of matter, a physical thing, may seem at first blush more likely to be determined than the conscious mind: it seems somehow more plausible that its development and its workings should be governed by the natural laws of cause and effect, so that any act which it initiates must also be so governed. But the theme of this book is that *all* human acts are governed in this way because free will really is nonsensical, and this brings us to the second of the two assumptions.

Determinism does *not* stand or fall according to whether our actions are initiated by the unconscious brain or by the conscious mind: it simply doesn't stand at all. If Libet's experiments, and all the others, had shown the exact opposite of what they did show - if, in other words, they showed that our acts are initiated by conscious decision, as everyone used to think they were - this would make no difference at all to the view of free will which this book puts forward. If neuroscientists think that it would make a difference to them, this goes perhaps to show that, before the experimental evidence hit them, they were just like everyone else in their uncritical acceptance of free will. The idea that consciousness is to be equated with free will or is bound somehow to embody or produce it, and that conscious initiation of an act is enough by itself to make it an act of free will, is a popular notion, but surely not a scientific one. (For all his striving to enlarge his patients' consciousness, Freud remained a determinist and never supposed that they had free will, still less that he was enlarging it.) The central problem about any act done in exercise of free will is that it must both reflect our character, our nature - show us for the people we are - and yet at the same time allow us to divorce ourselves from that character or nature and rise above it (or fall below it), doing so for no ascertainable reason. This paradox remains insoluble no matter whether the act is initiated by conscious mind or unconscious brain.

Perhaps neuroscientific investigation will in the end demonstrate conclusively that free will does not exist, and perhaps this conclusion will come to be generally accepted. Such books as this one will then become irrelevant. Meanwhile, in pursuing our investigations, we can usefully follow the advice offered to the public by the Second World War slogan: keep calm and carry on.

10.

What about falsifying predictions?

Determinism involves the consequence that a person's future actions could in principle be predicted – and that Laplace's Demon, with his all-embracing knowledge, could actually predict them. Take once more the example of Burglar Bill standing outside the house. We've assumed that he has a wholehearted desire to break in, and we ourselves feel quite confident that he will do so. But now suppose that we communicate this prediction to Bill himself. Might he not decide to falsify it out of sheer perversity and go home to bed? (We have to assume here that we make this communication in circumstances which do not of themselves affect his decision: if we were to do it by tapping him on the shoulder as he stood outside the house, we should certainly spoil the experiment.)

The answer to the question is that Bill might indeed decide to falsify our prediction, and might get quite a kick out of doing so. Does this show that he has free will? No, it doesn't, because in making our prediction we should be adding something to the causal chain, inserting into it another determining factor. Laplace's Demon could foresee this event and take it into account and, depending on his exhaustive knowledge of Bill's character, would make his own prediction accordingly. But if we pursue this line of thought a little further, we seem to come upon a strange paradox. Suppose that it is the Demon himself who makes the prediction which is communicated to Bill and that Bill, being the person he is, decides to prove it wrong and does so. The Demon's omniscience allows him to know that his prediction will be communicated to Burglar Bill. But if he knows this, he knows also that any prediction he may make will be invalidated by Bill deciding to do the opposite. So if he predicts a break-in, there won't be a break-in; and if he predicts no break-in, there will be a break-in. (This would not be so if Bill had a more acquiescent character, one which led him to fulfil the prediction instead of falsifying it, but nothing turns on that.) Does this show that human behaviour can't be predicted after all, even in principle? Does it disprove determinism and resurrect free will?

Suggestions have been made that our ability to falsify any prediction which may be communicated to us is indeed a proof or demonstration of free will. But this illustrates again the tendency to uphold free will by clutching at straws, because it just isn't so. On the contrary, it is the fact that Bill is told about the prediction which, taken in conjunction with his perverse character, determines his decision to break in or not to break in: this is a clear demonstration of determinism, not of free will. It may be that if Laplace's Demon existed in the real world and made public predictions, the predictions could be invalidated. But this is a characteristic of prediction, not of determinism, and it doesn't mean that, once the act occurs, its causes cannot (in principle) be traced back like those of any other act.

The whole scenario is of course fantastic in any case. When Laplace invented his Demon, he invented a hypothetical entity which stands outside the world and predicts its future. The invention was just a shorthand way of making a point about science, causality and natural laws. If Laplace's hypothesis had been that the Demon had a real existence in the real world, and therefore had to factor himself and his own doings into his predictions, it would have fallen apart at once and made Laplace a laughing stock.

11.

Do we form ourselves?

Up to now we have been considering an idea of free will which might be called free will *at the point of delivery*. This is the idea of it which nearly everyone has. If we say that someone's act or decision resulted from free will, what we mean is that his or her free will came into play at the time of the act or decision – that it was a freely willed act or decision. In Chapter 1, I recorded the two propositions in which, years ago, I summed up my own rejection of free will: *a person acts as he does because he is what he is; and he has not made himself what he is.* Up to now we have not paid much individual attention to the second of these propositions.

The view that the first proposition might be true without the second being true has always seemed to me quite untenable. Surely we can no more self-form than we can pull ourselves up by our own bootlaces. If we really did make ourselves what we are and form our own characters, it would have to be by means of a series of past acts, decisions, reactions and other mental activities of our own. And if our current activities are determined by our now-existing personalities, these bits of past activity must have been determined by our then-existing personalities. All these things are simply links in our causal chains. If free will is a nonsense concept at the time when Burglar Bill breaks into the house at the age of (say) twenty, it was equally a nonsense when he was deciding other things at the age of fifteen, ten or five. But now I want to introduce a philosopher who disagrees with this.

Ted Honderich, the determinist philosopher who comes and goes in these pages, has said that Professor Robert Kane "sometimes still seems to be at the head of the Free Will regiment" [21]. Professor Kane is University Distinguished Teaching Professor of Philosophy at the University of Texas at Austin. Among many other things, he is the editor of *Free Will*, part of the *Blackwell Readings in Philosophy* series [22]. The book contains a selection of writings on the subject of free will, and Professor Kane provides a general introduction and adds a commentary, raising difficulties and queries, to each contribution. My heart warms to him. His introduction charts brilliantly the hay which philosophers have made with this subject over the years and although he himself contributes a paper to the collection, *Free Will: New Directions for an Ancient Problem*, he treats it just the same as anyone else's, referring to himself in the third person as "Kane" and raising objections to it in his commentary.

In his paper, Professor Kane accepts that our ordinary, everyday acts and decisions really are determined by our existing personalities (and this, coming from a leading proponent of free will, is worth noticing), but he thinks that they can nonetheless be ascribed to "free will" because – or to the extent that – we have by past acts created our personalities for ourselves. This, of course, is not free will at the point of delivery. To most people, free will means that Burglar Bill, standing outside the house, really might decide to kick his burgling habit and go home. Professor Kane does not think this: he accepts that there is no chance of Bill acting against his wholehearted motivations in making what is, to him, an everyday decision like this, but he thinks that his breaking in can nonetheless be described as an act of free will because he has *made* the personality in which these motivations reside: he is the "ultimate creator" of his own personality. We could, at this point, bog ourselves down in the question whether, if this were so, it really would amount to free will or not, but let's leave that on one side and proceed to Professor Kane's ideas about self-creation. How does he think we do it?

We do it, he says, by means of past decisions which amount to "self-forming actions". He calls them "SFAs". A SFA occurs when, by being confronted with a particularly difficult or agonising kind of choice, we are "torn between competing visions of what we should do or become". To adapt an example which he gives, suppose that Sebastian is a high-flying business executive bent upon flying even higher. He is going to a meeting where his performance will be crucial to making an important advance in his career. But his route takes him along a lonely street where he sees a woman being knocked down and having her handbag stolen. He is late already, and if he stops to intervene - run after the thief, help the woman, call an ambulance, talk to the police - he will miss the meeting altogether. This kind of decision is so difficult and emotionally charged, says Professor Kane, that it stirs up "chaos" in Sebastian's brain. This sensitises the brain to "quantum indeterminacies at the neuronal level" and so opens "a window of opportunity that temporarily screens off *complete* determination by influences of the past." (The italics are mine.) Within this (partial) indeterminacy, Sebastian struggles to decide whether to stop and help the woman or go on to the meeting, wanting to do both things at once. Whichever alternative he chooses, the choice will involve him in overcoming his wish to adopt the other one. It will have been caused by his *efforts* and it will be a SFA. The element of indeterminacy is important to Kane's argument, but the indeterminacy isn't complete: it doesn't make Sebastian's choice a random choice but rather gives him the opportunity to make a choice which Kane claims to be self-forming. And once self-forming has occurred in this way, Sebastian's future actions can be ascribed to a self-formed personality and thus - and only thus - to be the products of free will. Professor Kane makes it quite clear that but for

SFAs there could in his view be no such thing as free will or moral responsibility.

I have tried to make a fair and accurate summary of Professor Kane's theory and I hope I've succeeded. To my mind, it provides a fascinating example of the kind of thing which philosophers get up to, particularly perhaps when they struggle to find some reason for believing in free will. But does it stand up to any sort of detached examination? Surely it comes apart in several different places.

To begin with, the theory rests largely on some puzzling assertions about physical events: it assumes implicitly that quantum indeterminacy in the microscopic world (at which we looked in Chapter 8) does not normally have any effect on the working of our brains, but that it does have an effect when some acute dilemma "sensitises" our brains to it, and that the effect which it then has is to "screen off" some (unspecified) part or parts of the determinative factors which would otherwise rule. None of these assertions seems to be self-evidently plausible. More important, however, is the great difficulty of grasping the conceptual nature of a SFA. According to Professor Kane, Sebastian's decision about the mugged woman is at least partially undetermined because of the chaos in his brain. But it is nonetheless very much a decision which he himself makes: otherwise it would not be a SFA. *Why* does he strive to make one choice and to reject the other? *Why* does he make the decision which he does make? Professor Kane says that the chaos in his brain temporarily and partially screens off the influences of the past (an assertion, incidentally, for which he seems to provide no evidence), but if Sebastian's motive force for his striving does not come from these influences, where on earth does it come from? I for one will not feel satisfied if this is to be treated simply as an unanswerable question. If Sebastian strives to go to the woman's aid, and does so, this must surely be because he *already* has a strong moral character and the influences which spring from it were *not* screened off. But

Professor Kane seems to doubt this. At all events, Sebastian's decision to help the woman is certainly a moral one: does it therefore reflect credit on him? One might think so, but this, too, seems doubtful. Yet surely Sebastian's decision can hardly generate moral responsibility for his future actions if it was not itself morally motivated and therefore creditable. And what effect on Sebastian's personality is his SFA supposed actually to have? If he is a moral and conscientious person before he takes a decision to stay and help the woman, then his good nature is the same after the decision as it was before: in what sense does it suddenly become self-created?

Another objection occurred to me as I read Professor Kane's paper, only to find that it had been raised by other philosophers and that he himself records it in his later commentary. Imagine the existence of two identical people, Sebastian One and Sebastian Two, confronted by two identical choices in identical circumstances. If their choices really are *not* determined, it follows that one might make one choice and the other the other. Surely this cannot be ascribed to anything but what Professor Kane calls "luck" (whatever exactly that may be). And luck can hardly to equated with free will or provide a foundation for it.

But let us end with an objection which seems not to be addressed either in Professor Kane's article or in his commentary. How many SFAs does it take to self-form a personality? It can't be suggested, surely, that Sebastian's one SFA is sufficient to do this. Different kinds of SFA must be needed to self-form different parts of the personality. One personality is the repository for an almost infinitely complex mesh of emotions, motives, drives, prohibitions, and so on. Surely the entirety cannot be self-formed by a dozen SFAs, let alone by one. And if Sebastian's SFAs form the foundation for his free will and moral responsibility in taking some particular decision in the future, as Kane asserts, then surely there must be, among those SFAs, at least one which is somehow *relevant* to that future decision. It's hard to see how Sebastian's decision about the mugged woman has any bearing on, or makes him morally responsible for, a future decision as to whether to give his wife a diamond brooch or a paperback book for her birthday, or even to make or to refuse a donation to the Society for the Protection of Tame Rats. Are we to suppose that particular kinds of SFA generate responsibility only for corresponding kinds of future decision, so that other future decisions still remain fully determined and involve no responsibility at all?

And is it actually a foregone conclusion that all of us have, during our past lives, had the need to take SFAs, or a sufficient number of them? What if our lives have been so tranquil that, at least up to now, we haven't had to do so? And tranquillity is not the only thing which might preclude SFAs. Let's return once more to Burglar Bill. We've assumed that his heredity and environment have left him with a lot of anti-social feelings and not much in the way of a normal conscience. Can you imagine any situations in which he has been torn between competing visions of what he should do or become? Even if Professor Kane's theory were correct it couldn't possibly provide a means of deciding whether any given person has, or has not, been forced by circumstances into the SFAs which were required to create responsibility for any particular action in the future.

But surely, and with enormous respect to Professor Kane, his theory is simply not sustainable. It is really supported by little more than wishful thinking. There is nothing in it to dispel determinism or, if you prefer, determinism and chance - or, as perhaps Professor Kane himself (or his other critics) might prefer, determinism and luck.

12.

Can the human mind
evaluate free will?

It is impossible to prove conclusively that the human mind is capable of dealing with anything at all. No philosophical proposition, no proposition of any kind, not even an assertion that night follows day, can be conclusively shown to be true because all are in theory vulnerable to this fact. We cannot prove that our minds make sense rather than nonsense, because our only means of doing this would involve us in using and relying on our minds, and so we should be assuming what we set out to prove. But this ultimate uncertainty is something which has to be ignored. Otherwise Ludwig Wittgenstein's aphorism, "Whereof one cannot speak thereof one must be silent", would have universal application. Or would it? If the human mind doesn't make sense, then every statement you make would invalidate itself the moment you made it - before you made it. But even that statement may not make sense. And neither may that. And neither may that. You can't even be sure that you can't be sure. Or can you? There is simply no way forward. Or is there? You are lost. Or aren't you?

Even if, in order to live in what we take to be the real world, we must assume that our minds do make sense - and it certainly seems that they must make sufficient sense to enable us to live in that world - it is still possible to think that they may be incapable of making sense of certain particular things. In Chapter 9 we noticed

Colin McGinn's suggestion that the human mind is incapable of resolving the mind-brain problem. Some have said the same about the problem of free will. In 1788 the great German philosopher Immanuel Kant (1724-1804) said that there were only three things beyond the power of human intellect: God, immortality and free will. (The mind-brain problem did not figure in his list.)

The first point to make here is that the free will-determinism problem (if problem it is) is not *like* the mind-brain problem. That problem is a genuinely difficult one: there really is no way (in the light of present knowledge) of understanding the exact relation in which mind and brain stand to one another, and when McGinn says that the human mind is not equipped to understand it, he is not making any assumptions, or coming from anywhere in particular: he is just standing perplexed in front of the problem because nothing seems to him to fit. But people who say that the human mind cannot understand free will are usually people who are committed to free will and are bent upon defending it from rational attack. Free will and determinism are a pair of alternatives: free will is indeed incomprehensible, but determinism is not, and the sensible conclusion to draw from this is that free will doesn't exist and determinism does. The fact that you can't make sense of free will is not a problem unless you can't bear to stop believing in it. The fact that we cannot comprehend it is attributable, not to the limitations of our intellect, but to its *intrinsic* incomprehensibility.

If, as human beings, we need to make a choice which has practical implications – and the choice between free will and determinism does have practical implications – what we normally do is to apply as best we can such intelligence as we can muster in order to come down on one side or the other. We don't do this in relation to free will and determinism, but surely it is high time we did. We wouldn't apply to anything else the "hands off" approach which we take to free will. We don't see the limitations of the human mind as a reason for thinking that two and two make five. We don't see the incomprehensibility of fairies as a reason for believing in them. It is only when we come to free will and determinism that we jump the irrational way, instead of the rational one, and we do this because of our emotional commitment to free will.

But perhaps it is wrong to say "only". What, for example, about the other two members of Kant's trio: God and immortality? Surely we apply exactly the same "hands off" approach to these things as we apply to free will, taking their incomprehensibility as giving them a sort of added lustre, even an added credibility. Or we did. Our emotional commitment to the ideas of God and immortality was once every bit as strong as our commitment to that of free will, but it is no longer unthinkable for very many people to subject these two ideas to rational analysis and to treat their incomprehensibility as a reason, not for believing in them, but for rejecting them – to assert that God and immortality are incomprehensible, not because the human mind is limited, but because they don't exist. It is not necessary to my argument for me to assert that such people are right: my point is only that if we can adopt this different attitude to these two sacred subjects, we can surely adopt it also to the equally sacred subject of free will.

★ ★ ★ ★ ★

In Chapter 3, I examined the idea of free will and came to the conclusion that it seemed to be a self-evidently nonsensical one. The aim of Part II of the book has been to consider the arguments which might be advanced in its favour, or in favour of some more sensible conception of it, and to see whether any of these might serve to rescue it. If you think that any of them may do this, or that other arguments might do so, you will hang on to that belief without my encouragement, but I offer it nonetheless. For myself, however, I think that all attempts at rescue have failed and, as this part draws to a close, I have to say that the idea of free will seems to me no less nonsensical.

PART III

DO WE REALLY BELIEVE IN FREE WILL?

13.

Our ambivalence

"You are a dangerous man," said the judge. Judges often inform convicted offenders of their dangerousness just before they sentence them to a term of imprisonment designed to protect the public from its effects. A thief who stole a car and ran over and seriously injured a mother who was scraping ice from its windscreen was told recently that he was so dangerous that he might never be released [23]. What do judges mean when they say things like this? Evidently they have formed a view of the offender's character, based on the offence he has committed and perhaps on past offences as well, and concluded that it will lead him to commit similar offences in the future unless he is safely tucked away in prison. And very likely the judges are absolutely right. Yet they are not embracing determinism and rejecting free will – at least not consciously. The idea of free will is central to the criminal law, and the judges quite clearly believe that the offender might, by exercising his own free will, have refrained from committing the offence of which he has been convicted and any other offences on which their view of him is based. Their condemnation of him amounts to blame for not having done so: the car thief's judge called him "absolutely despicable".

So don't we have something of a contradiction here? Why does a judge assume that someone who has proved dangerous in the past will go on being dangerous in the future? If he might, by exercising his free will, have avoided his past crimes, why might he not, by the same means, avoid any future ones, so abstaining from behaviour which is not only destructive but self-destructive? Is the judge saying implicitly that the offender has free will but can be relied on not to exercise it, or that he has free will but can be relied on to exercise it only so as to act out his criminal propensities? These ideas come to the same thing and neither makes any sense. Both assume that, though the offender has free will, it will not be exercised with any effect; and a free will of which this is true is not a free will at all. And the judges, whether they realise it or not, are endorsing this view.

And Parliament has endorsed it too. For example, section 225 of the Criminal Justice Act 2003 introduced a new sentence called "imprisonment for public protection" ("IPP" for short). Under these provisions, the sentence which an offender would otherwise receive must, in specified circumstances, be increased to one of life imprisonment if the court foresees "a significant risk to members of the public of serious harm occasioned by the commission by him of further specified offences". Section 225 came into force in April 2005 and by 2009, according to a decision of the House of Lords, the resulting increase in life sentences had "swamped the prison system" [24]. At the time of writing, a question mark hangs over the future of the IPP legislation, but this is because of the swamping, not because the court's supposed ability to predict an offender's future behaviour is seen to be inconsistent with his having free will.

Another example of this tendency was provided in 2010 by the reaction of the Prime Minister, David Cameron, to a decision of the Supreme Court (which has now replaced the House of Lords in its judicial capacity). Under the then existing law, certain sex offenders had to comply, for the whole of the rest of their lives, with a notification procedure requiring them (among other things) to tell the police whenever they changed their address. The Supreme Court, recognising that some offenders might in later years have made so much progress as no longer to pose any threat, decided that the Human Rights Act 1998 [25] required them to be given some opportunity to demonstrate this and so bring the notification procedure to an end. David Cameron [26] was "appalled" by this decision, called it "completely offensive" and said that it "flies in the face of common sense". His reaction seems likely to embody two contradictory ideas. One is a sort of misapplied or exaggerated determinism ("once an sex offender, always a sex offender" seems to have been his underlying thought): a belief that such reformative measures as Government might provide could never result in actual reform. But the force of his denunciation seems also to show a strong dislike of sex offenders which I think he would have sought to justify, if pressed, on the basis that their crimes were not determined but freely willed.

There is nothing new in the idea that people can harbour two diametrically opposed beliefs at the same time, acting in some circumstances on the one and in other circumstances on the other. One, or even both, of these beliefs may be conscious, half conscious or unconscious, but both are potent. And the best, biggest and most remarkable example of this syndrome is provided by the subject matter of this book. It isn't just judges, legislators and Prime Ministers who harbour this ambivalence: we all do.

If free will existed it would mean that, although our personality may be determined, this determined personality does not determine our behaviour because free will allows us always to transcend it. Our behaviour may be constrained because some of the things which we would otherwise do are physically impossible, either for people in general or for us in particular. It may equally be constrained by our mental capacity: the most ardent proponents of free will would not suggest that someone with a low I.Q. is free to become a rocket scientist, or that someone with a recognised mental illness is free to behave quite normally. And nowadays most (perhaps not quite all) of those proponents would accept that it is constrained by a sexual

71

orientation which is to a large extent if not entirely inbuilt. But although our behaviour may be constrained in these ways, a true proponent of free will would maintain – must maintain – that it is not otherwise constrained by our personalities and the preponderance of motivation within them. Such a proponent must maintain that, despite everything, Burglar Bill really might decide not to break in – and that, no matter how certain Laplace's Demon might feel about our future behaviour, we might prove him wrong time and time again.

But if free will did exist, with anything like the implications just described, then it would invalidate pretty much the whole of psychology, psychiatry, criminology, sociology and any other science or system you can think of which concerns itself with human behaviour. All these disciplines assume that it is possible to say things about one person's behaviour which will be relevant also to the behaviour of another person of the same type; that particular kinds of people behave in particular ways; that it is possible to speak of, and even to discover, the origins of a person's behaviour; that it is possible, on the basis of assessment, study and investigation, to understand someone and to predict, in the light of that understanding, how they will behave and how their behaviour might perhaps be modified. In short, they all assume that human behaviour results from factors which can be explored – that it is *caused*. They all assume what a single-minded proponent of free will could not accept: that people's behaviour, and their thoughts and feelings, are the result of their pre-existing personalities, which in turn are the result of the hereditary and environmental factors which have gone to create them. And none of these disciplines could offer us any help – none of them would exist at all – if free will ruled.

"Tough on crime and tough on the causes of crime": you recall New Labour's old slogan? Why did this not seem nonsensical to anyone, because surely it should have done? If criminals really and truly have free will, crime doesn't *have* causes. An article in *The Times* in March 2007 was headed, "Myra Hindley: the childhood that created a murderess". It is unlikely that any reader was affronted, or even surprised, by this heading, but doesn't it amount to an affirmation of determinism and a rejection of free will? Did the writer realise this? Almost certainly not, any more than most readers did. And these examples are typical of innumerable instances in which, tacitly and probably without admitting it to ourselves, but quite unequivocally, we take determinism for granted.

But what about the other side of the coin, the contrary belief which goes to make the ambivalence? Are we really happy to accept that Myra Hindley did what she did simply because her childhood had made her a murderess and so determined her crimes? (This of course is an over-simplification because her heredity played its part, and the environmental factors which interacted with it were probably far more complex than the journalist supposed, but let that pass.) The answer is that most of us would be deeply unhappy to accept this and very angry to have it suggested. Most people will cling tenaciously, even desperately, to the idea of free will when confronted by a case like Myra Hindley's, or indeed by any concrete example of a person behaving in a way which is violent, cruel, hurtful and destructive. Because Myra Hindley was "evil" and "wicked", wasn't she? Don't I believe in evil, in wickedness? Well, yes and no. If you want to label conduct like hers, because it is done for selfish reasons and causes terrible suffering, as proceeding from evil and wickedness, by all means label it in that way. But to do this doesn't seem to tell us anything about it. It doesn't even smack very strongly of free will, because if you attribute Myra Hindley's acts to evil and wickedness you're not really attributing them to *her*, and in any case it remains to ask where she got the evil and wickedness from. But of course the labelling, and the condemnation that goes with it, are meant to put a stop to such questions. If someone is wicked or evil, that is an end of the matter. You're not supposed to ask how they got to be that way: you're meant to assume that they got to be that way because they woke up one morning and freely (but for no reason) decided to be that way. The concepts of evil and wickedness amount to a smokescreen, or a barrier, which is not to be penetrated.

An example of this is provided by the description in the *Radio Times* of a programme, *Interview with a Serial Killer*, shown in 2009 [27]: "The programme explores the reasons behind his crimes, and asks whether he was an evil man who enjoyed killing for his own pleasure, or if he was the victim of brain damage and childhood abuse." These two possibilities are presented as mutually exclusive alternatives. If he was an evil man, you look no further for his reasons. If he was not, then and only then are you allowed to seek them in such things as brain damage and abuse. And if it is the taking of pleasure from his crimes that would make him evil, what if it was brain damage or childhood abuse which caused him to take the pleasure?

The truth is that we want to have it both ways. I wonder whether, even if you are a wholehearted believer in free will, you might have felt inclined to back away a little from the description of it which appeared earlier in this chapter. "Perhaps I wouldn't go quite as far as that," you might have said, "but ...". Many people would want to try, by this means, to have their cake and eat it. They don't really want to consign all the behavioural sciences to oblivion. They don't really want to discount the idea that heredity and environment may predispose a person to crime (or saintliness). But they still want to think that free will must exist somewhere because if they didn't they might end up having to treat someone like Myra Hindley as a product of causality instead of treating her as an evil witch. So might it be possible to find some compromise between free will and determinism, some means by which we really can have it both ways? This is explored in the next chapter.

14.

Just a little bit ... not too much of it?

Has it occurred to anyone who has read the earlier parts of this book to wonder whether, in my description of free will, I am setting up an artificial Aunt Sally just for the fun of knocking it down? Do you feel, perhaps, that I have exaggerated the effect which free will is supposed to have? Have you sometimes felt inclined to say, "Oh, well, of course I don't believe in *complete* free will. That would be silly. But I'm sure that people have *some* free will. There must be a little bit of free will in there somewhere"?

The kind of free will with which this book has been concerned is the one to which we were led in Chapter 3 - the popular idea of it, the kind of free will which most people have in their minds, however vaguely, when they think about it; the kind of free will which is thought to justify the retributive punishment inherent in the criminal law; the kind of free will which (as we shall see in Chapter 18) Kant wanted to find in what he called the *noumenon*; the kind of free will which lets us see our natural anger as righteous anger. This is the kind of free will which would enable us to say that, by virtue of it, Burglar Bill could and might walk away from the house, and that Myra Hindley could and might have refrained from the terrible crimes which she committed. No other conception of free will can bear the weight which we, as a society and as individuals, seek to put upon it.

But this idea of free will is self-evidently hard to uphold: Burglar

Bill, with his wholehearted desire to break into the house, turning away, doing so for no ascertainable reason, and getting blamed if he doesn't. Or take an example from the other end of the spectrum. Cardinal Basil Hume was, by all accounts, a very good and kindly man. When he was Archbishop of Westminster he used to walk at night through the streets around the Cathedral. Suppose that on one of these walks he came upon an old lady lying on a pavement, obviously ill or injured, barely conscious but still alive. The street is deserted. There is no one to see him. Is he going to reassure her, try to make her comfortable, get help … or is he going to kick her savagely in the head and go on his way smiling? We feel so sure of the answer that we think the question stupid and insulting: surely, if he took the second course, it could only be because of some sudden, catastrophic, pathological event in his brain. But suppose there was no such event and that he did take that course nonetheless, and suppose that his crime was discovered. Imagine a newspaper headline: *"I don't know what came over me," says Archbishop, "it must have been free will".* The idea that, because of free will, the Cardinal Archbishop of Westminster might kick an old lady to death is incredible, but it is actually no more incredible than that someone with Burglar Bill's motivations might turn away from the empty house and lead a law-abiding life. Yet this is the sort of effect which, every day, we expect free will to achieve.

So it really is tempting to look for some way of lowering these unrealistic expectations of free will while still maintaining its existence – of finding some sort of compromise. Could we think of free will as a faculty which sometimes operates and sometimes doesn't, like a failing light bulb which flickers on and off? Or perhaps we could see it as a faculty which, though constant, is of limited power, operating only within a limited range, strong enough to do some things but too weak to do others? At the beginning of the twentieth century, the music hall artist Marie Lloyd was singing a song called *When I take my morning promenade*. Part of the chorus went

> Do you think my dress is a little bit
> Just a little bit … Well not too much of it
> Though it shows my shape just a little bit
> That's the little bit the boys admire.

If we could find some basis for the idea that we all have a little bit of free will, but not too much of it - not enough to make the whole concept ridiculous - boys and girls of all ages might well admire it.

After I had finished the last but one draft of this book I did something which I had determined not to do but which it was evidently determined that I should do and read another philosophical treatment of free will and determinism [28]. The author, a professor of philosophy, sought to show that determinism does not apply to human beings. He was kind enough to exchange some messages with me when I approached him after reading the book, and I was grateful. That he made no response to my last message was less surprising than his kindness in responding to the others. But his arguments against determinism seemed to me wholly unconvincing. Some didn't begin to stand up. For example, he drew attention more than once to the fact that people with "very similar" upbringings may become very different people, seeming to think this an obvious disproof of determinism. Surely research into heredity cannot have passed him by? He must know that people are born with widely differing hereditary endowments and that these will be as important in forming their characters as the environmental factors which bear upon them as they are brought up – and indeed will largely determine the different ways in which they react to these factors? And how similar, anyway, is "similar"? This, with respect, is not many miles away from the sort of argument you might expect from the bloke down the pub.

But enough of that. The real interest of the book doesn't lie in what it says about determinism. It doesn't actually lie in what it says about anything: it lies in what it doesn't say. Although the phrase "Free Will" forms its title, the book does not at any point describe, still less define, this concept. It sets out to rescue free will from determinism, but readers are never told what the free will thus rescued might actually amount to. The author assumes (as many philosophers seem to do) that it is a coherent concept which requires no description, examination or justification. But when I ventured to press him on this point, taking Myra Hindley as an example, it emerged that the professor's idea of free will was not at all the idea which I described at the start of this chapter. There is, he said, a lot less free will than many people hope or imagine. His idea is of a severely limited free will, operating only within a range of possibilities which cannot be defined but is certainly narrow. He is, in other words, a real life subscriber to the idea of the little bit of free will in there somewhere. He doubted whether, as the moment approached for Myra Hindley to commit a crime, his version of free will would have allowed her to refrain from it. He said that, because of "who she had become" it might have been very "difficult" for her to refrain, and that no one is entitled to say that she could have done so. And of course Myra Hindley is not alone in being the person she has become: as I have tried to argue already, perhaps at tedious length, each and every one of us is the person we have become.

Two fatal blows must be aimed at this idea of a limited, partial, meagre or downsized free will. The first is to assert that it really makes no sense. If the idea of full free will is incoherent, then the idea of "a little bit of free will in there somewhere" is equally incoherent and perhaps more so. You can't dispose of the arguments against free will just by lowering the stakes – any more than the unmarried mother who had the unplanned baby could change anything by saying that it was only a little one. Even if our free will is fettered so that it provides us, not with an open playing field, but only with a certain amount of "wriggle room", we still have to ask the questions which were asked towards the end of Chapter 3. Let us invent a character called Terence and suppose that he decides to do some particular act rather than to refrain from it, and that this decision is within his own personal wriggle room. Can we not still ask why he wriggled in the direction of doing it, rather than in the direction of not doing it? The professor's book says that defenders of free will do not wish human actions to be "mysterious", but to be *explicable* in terms of "motives … and such like" [29]. No doubt they do, but they can't have it both ways and their wish is doomed to disappointment, because if the mystery is to be dispelled by an explanation in terms of "motives and such like", the explanation has to be a causal explanation which anchors Terence's act to his personality – an explanation which tells us something about Terence as a person – and this is necessarily a deterministic explanation.

The second blow which must be aimed at the "wriggle room" idea of free will is this. To say that Terence has a facility called free will is to do no more than to pin a meaningless label on him unless that facility connotes a clear ability to make and act upon choices different from the ones which he actually makes and acts upon; and the professor cannot say that it does or, if it does, when it does or the extent to which it does. If the facility amounted only to a little bit of free will in there somewhere, then it would not enable us to draw any useful conclusions whatever about any particular piece of human behaviour, because we wouldn't be able to tell whether that behaviour was due to that little bit or to the determinism which otherwise ruled. For all practical purposes you might just as well write free will off altogether as suppose that we have only a little bit of it. And this point needs to be strongly emphasised because an idea of *limited* free will is something of a Trojan Horse. If it is once accepted, those who put it forward are more than likely to act from then onwards as if they had won the battle and established free will in a full and potent sense - as if their little bit amounted to the whole lot. And this, it seems to me, is exactly what, in his book, the professor does.

PART IV

IMPLICATIONS OF DISBELIEF

15.

Reason and emotion

To set the scene for this part of the book, we need to remind ourselves of something which, though it really is of great importance, is often overlooked. Human beings are not motivated by reason. When, at the end of the nineteenth century, A.N. Whitehead and Bertrand Russell were collaborating on their *Principia Mathematica*, taking over 350 pages to prove that $1+1=2$ and going on to produce three massive volumes, they demonstrated to an extraordinary degree the intellectual capacity of the human mind, but it was not their intellects which motivated them to do it. Their purpose was to show that all mathematics is in some sense reducible to logic, and they pursued that objective *because they wanted to*. The achievement at which they aimed was one which would satisfy emotional desires within them: without these they would have had just as much intelligence but they would not have used it in this way. Without *some* emotional motivation, none of us would use our intelligence at all. It's true of course that a few people seem to have a simple love of intellectual exploration, but it is in the love and not the intellect that their motives are to be found: what does the exploration mean to them and why do they love it?

If we could manage for a moment to detach ourselves from our feelings about free will and determinism, and look at these two concepts objectively, wouldn't determinism seem a pretty unsurprising, natural and ordinary idea, and wouldn't free will seem a very strange one? So why do we habitually see the situation the other way around: why do so many of us accept free will without thinking about it, and have so much difficulty in accepting determinism? The answer surely lies largely in the fact that reason and the intellect are not motivating forces within the personality: they will take us from A to B (and B may be a destination as yet unknown), but they will do so only if we want to make the journey. Towards the end of Chapter 10, I said: "It is only when we come to free will and determinism that we jump the irrational way, instead of the rational one, and we do this because of our emotional commitment to free will."

A relative of mine expressed her surprise at the fact that people like the then Archbishop of Canterbury should be religious believers because, as she put it with a rising note of surprise in her voice, they are intelligent people. She thought the Christian religion an obvious nonsense and was surprised that all intelligent people couldn't see this. It does not matter for present purposes whether she was right about religion. But *if* she was right – if reason really does lead the dispassionate observer to the conclusion at which she had arrived – the fact that the Archbishop of Canterbury and others don't agree with her is still not at all surprising. For conscious or unconscious reasons, they would not encourage their intellects to make this journey. It was one of the royal Dukes, since deceased, who, in an endearing moment, said that he had never had any doubts about religion, but that he probably would have had if he had been more intelligent. Well, only up to a point, your Royal Highness: if religious belief is sufficiently ingrained, if it brings you comfort, if you see it as wisdom received from people you respect and trust and you have made it a fundamental part of your life, then, however intelligent you may be, you probably won't have the motivation to set out on any intellectual journey which might take you away from it. Perhaps you won't even see that such a journey is possible and perhaps, in your case, it isn't.

What is true of religious belief is true also of belief in free will. There is no attempt here to tie the two together except by way of analogy, because atheists can believe in free will just as Christians can believe (and in the past have believed) in determinism. The point is that if belief in free will is ingrained and brings satisfaction and is a fundamental part of your approach to life, then (just as in the case of religion) you probably won't want to set out on an intellectual journey which may end in your rejecting it. You might find it hard to the point of impossibility to define what free will *is*, just as Christians find it very hard to define what God is, but this is an intellectual question and you probably have no desire to engage with it. The emotional resistance to the idea of determinism is a far more potent obstacle in the way of its acceptance than any of the intellectual difficulties which people may think they have with it. In fact these intellectual difficulties, or some of them, may well be substitutes, covers or fronts for the emotional resistance.

16.

What have we got to lose?

To many people determinism seems alarming, even threatening. Partly this is due to a misunderstanding of its nature.

As we've noticed, it isn't to be seen as some malign and alien force which we struggle in vain to overcome, but rather as a natural process which works through us and not against us. It is also, of course, a process of which we are largely unaware. And although the future may be an ineluctable result of the past, we do not know – and can never know – what it actually holds. Some people, and even some philosophers who are determinists, say they find determinism depressing. One such philosopher, Ted Honderich, is on record as saying that it sometimes "gets him down". I do find this hard to understand.

It's true of course that the chains of causality which are already being forged will determine the outcome of our hopes about the future, fulfilling some and frustrating others (or, conceivably, fulfilling or frustrating the whole lot) but we have no idea what the outcome is to be. If we were Laplace's Demon, perhaps we should know that some of our hopes (or perhaps all of our hopes) would always be unfulfilled, and that would certainly be a sad state of affairs; but we are not Laplace's Demon and we do not know. The future is just as closed to us as if there were no such thing as determinism. When we watch a film or see a play or read a novel, we know that every bit of the story it tells is already fixed - indeed, is already in existence and already known to some people if not yet to us - but this does not reduce in any way our eagerness to follow its twists and turns and to know how it ends. Nor should belief in determinism affect us as we live our lives, or discourage us from doing what we would otherwise be doing: striving towards our objectives. It may be that all our striving will be in vain, but that has to be true anyway, doesn't it?

Another perceived difficulty which determinism may pose for some people is that it seems to have a sort of circular effect. If whatever I do is determined, they say to themselves, I might as well give up, sit doing nothing, get drunk every night, steal from my employer, gamble away all my money ... because whatever I do it must have been determined that I should do it. Well, this may literally be true, but a belief in determinism isn't going to change your personality and it certainly isn't going to save you from the consequences of your actions. There are some respects in which a belief in determinism might affect your attitudes to other people or to society's institutions – more about this later – but it isn't going to plunge you into despair or turn you into a criminal or an uncaring hedonist. Determinism is a intellectual concept and people aren't driven by their intellects.

Others may perceive determinism in the opposite way, by supposing it to mean that people cannot change. (Bertrand Russell's biographer, mentioned at the start of Chapter 6, seems to have harboured this view.) They say to themselves: if it's determined that I'm the way I am, my nature determined, the course of my life determined, what can I do about it? Well, we know that it really is difficult for people to change (and this in itself may be a pointer towards determinism, because if there were free will it would presumably be easier). But there is a confusion here. It is certainly implicit in determinism that you won't change unless it is determined that you should, but it may *be* determined that you should, and no one knows whether this is so or not. If you wish to change, this may be a pretty good indication that (perhaps with help) you will manage to do so [30]: evidently the seeds of change are already there and there's nothing in determinism to discourage you from doing what you would do anyway and having a try. Determinists, after all, go about their everyday lives like anybody else. It is determined that I try to write this book (I should be saved a lot of trouble if it weren't); if the book has any effect at all, that effect will be determined; and if it should change anyone's view about free will, it will do so by playing a part in the causality which leads to that person's changed view.

But these concerns are overshadowed by a more fundamental one: that belief in free will plays so important a part in our society, our institutions, our culture, our moral values, our sense of selfhood, our feelings about other people, our whole emotional life, that we simply cannot discard it. To do so would amount, more or less, to the end of civilisation as we know it. There certainly seems to be a widespread reluctance to press the case against free will. Many philosophers, neuroscientists and others disbelieve in it but they seem to do so rather quietly: it is as if they don't want their disbelief to go beyond the groves of academe and into the world of everyday. Perhaps they don't want to be identified too strongly with an unpopular message or perhaps they themselves share the concerns just mentioned. These concerns are addressed individually in later chapters of this book, but here we need to make one general point about them.

To believe in free will because you think it exists is one thing. Although this book has sought to show the contrary, its arguments are of course open to refutation by anyone who is minded to refute them. But to maintain or encourage belief in free will because, whether it exists or not, you think people can't get by without it, is something else again. Every so often letters, reports and articles appear in the newspapers lamenting the decline in religious belief.

They seek to identify the sad consequences of this decline and to assert that things were better in various ways when religious observance was strong and widespread. This may or may not be true, but the point to notice is that the approach of those who say these things is a wholly utilitarian one: they seek to advance religious belief, not on the ground that religion is true and our immortal souls are in danger if we reject it, but on the ground that it improves behaviour – that it is a kind of medicine which makes us better. (Karl Marx may have been saying rather the same thing from the opposite point of view when he described it as the opium of the people.) This approach can hardly fail to irritate atheists and agnostics, but it is also a deeply patronising one. The idea that someone knows better than you what you ought to believe is unpalatable.

And this, surely, is why we cannot accept the utilitarian view that we must believe in free will because disbelief will have ill consequences. You may say, justly, that I have an axe to grind, because the very existence of this book would, on that view, have to be condemned. But if the human race is to drag itself towards better things (and no one in their right mind would doubt that it needs to) a great deal must surely depend on our ability and willingness to face reality, to concern ourselves with the people and events that move around us and to understand them realistically. To accept that we must forever maintain a conspiracy of silence about some important aspect of our existence would be demeaning. And "conspiracy of silence" is the right phrase to use here. What *is* it, after all, that we are meant to go on believing in? Is this a forbidden question? The theme of this book is that free will, once examined, turns out to be a nonsensical idea, and if this is right then belief can be maintained only by not examining it. When I was a child my father gave me a huge picture, mounted on three folding cardboard panels, of a landscape full of woods and mountains, castles and houses, seas, rivers and winding paths, in which the characters and settings from fairy stories and nursery rhymes were shown and named: "This is the house that Jack built", "Tom Tom the piper's son ran this way", "Here old King Cole lives". But one of the paths ended only in a black hole in the hillside and the words, "Do not go in here". Is this the injunction which we should apply to an examination of free will? Is there really an unnamed horror lurking in this hole? Or does free will itself belong in a fairy story which, sooner or later, we shall outgrow?

None of this is meant to imply that a lifting of the injunction would automatically result in the rejection of free will: far from it. The fact that belief in free will seems to satisfy emotional needs, and the obstacle which this presents to its rejection, have been noted already and will be looked at again later on. But before this chapter ends, let's return to the thought with which it started: that determinism seems alarming or threatening. The first point to make is that if free will doesn't exist, then determinism *itself* cannot be alarming or threatening because we have been living with it unawares since the human race began. And *belief* in determinism is surely no more threatening than determinism itself: we don't have to respond to it in any way at all if we don't want to. Our emotions have primacy over our intellectual beliefs and this particular belief would not *force* changes upon us.

One final thought. The view that free will is a familiar and comforting concept, and determinism an alien and alarming one, surely becomes untenable if we can bring ourselves to analyse the idea of free will. Our allegiance to the idea depends entirely upon a refusal to look it full in the face. This allegiance depends upon fudges, on fuzziness, on hidden contradictions which we choose to ignore and on implicit compromises and accommodations which would fall apart if they were examined. Real free will – the free will in which we profess to believe but really don't believe, free will shorn of all the obfuscations, free will strong enough to support the weight of what we try to build upon it – *that* free will would surely be a glimpse of insanity. Comfort would lie in determinism.

17.

Determinism and morality

A contemporary philosopher who maintains a belief in free will, basing himself on the very individual approach of the philosopher Immanuel Kant (already mentioned briefly in Chapters 3 and 12), makes some rather dogmatic assertions about determinism [31]. He says that if it is true then all moral propositions are false. A determinist, he says, is "under a logical obligation to expunge every such falsehood from his own discourse and thinking, indeed from his whole conception of the world – all concepts of fairness, justice, praise or blame, good or bad, right or wrong, all morally evaluative terms whatsoever, in so far as they are ever applied to human beings and their actions, not only as individuals but through institutions."

Wow. I'm not sure what a "logical obligation" is, but let us address ourselves to the substance of these assertions. Kant does indeed maintain that all moral concepts depend upon the existence of free will. It was Kant who (as recorded in Chapter 12) said that free will was one of the three things which were beyond the power of the human intellect. It might perhaps have been better if he had left it at that, but what he actually did was to suggest that it existed, not in our everyday world, but in what he called the *noumenon* (more of that later).

But to maintain that morality must stand or fall with the existence of free will is to ignore completely the realities of human life and human motivation. If all goes reasonably well with a child's upbringing (and quite often it doesn't) some things are built into his or her personality. These include the conscience, which is the source of moral *feeling*, and this inbuilt conscientious restraint of harmful behaviour – behaviour about which the child is brought up to feel guilty and ashamed – is essential to our civilised existence, just as an inbuilt restraint on jumping off cliffs or running across busy roads is essential to our personal existence. This is why our ethos and our institutions are directed to its inculcation. And it is from this inbuilt moral feeling that moral concepts derive, not *vice versa*. To suggest that all this must fall by the wayside because of an intellectual acceptance of determinism is to put the cart a long way before the horse. Morality is an essential part of human existence and we have it, not because it is justified by the existence of free will in the noumenon, but because we need it and couldn't possibly do without it. Our morality is dictated by the *ends* it needs to serve.

Whatever the precise means by which it has done so, evolution has given us the capacity for what we call moral feelings, and (no pun intended) a good thing too. The concepts which the philosopher has listed, and a few others which he could have added, are all based in one way or another upon these moral feelings and, whether or not they can be justified philosophically, they can certainly be justified pragmatically because moral feelings are essential to civilisation and these concepts express, uphold, reinforce and further them. Determinists know that we can't help having acquired the personalities which lead us to do the things we do and that we do not *deserve* to be praised or blamed for doing these things, but they know also that this is not a good or sufficient reason (and would indeed be a hopelessly bad reason) for withholding expressions of approval or admiration, disapproval or condemnation from those who do them.

There is after all nothing unusual in admiring or condemning characteristics which a person cannot help having. When we express our admiration of people for being clever, beautiful or creative or, if we are cruel, condemn them for being ugly, stupid or unimaginative, we know perfectly well that they have played no part in creating these characteristics, but this fact alone doesn't stop us. And by the same token we can admire people for being good, or condemn them for being bad, even if we are determinists and know quite well that these characteristics, too, have been foisted on them by outside forces. It could indeed be argued that we are all the more justified (at least pragmatically) in doing this if the characteristics in question are moral, because there is then a possibility that what we say may lead to more good behaviour, or to less bad behaviour. Our task is to encourage the good and to discourage the bad, and this is a way to do it. No one has ever been made cleverer by being told they are stupid, but it really is possible to make people better by expressing our approval or disapproval of their behaviour because these reactions of ours are added to the chain of causality which determines their behaviour in the future.

Let's look at one particular concept, which might appear to be of overarching importance: that of "moral responsibility". Many people who oppose the idea of determinism seem to have at the back (or perhaps even at the front) of their minds the fear that it negates or precludes moral responsibility – and if we aren't morally responsible for our behaviour, what then? Is there to be chaos; are we all going to fall into the abyss? Philosophers have probably spent as much time in trying to deal with this concept as in dealing with anything else at all. So what are we to say about it?

Most of us, whether or not we are determinists, know what it is like to *feel* responsible for something. And all of us know what it is like to be *held* responsible for something. Neither of these things, of course, is the same as actually *being* responsible for the something, but perhaps that doesn't matter too much. A *feeling* of responsibility for one's actions is an emotion to which most people (but by no means all) are subject, and belief in determinism isn't going to take it away from them. Whether this feeling takes the form of guilt, or of regret or remorse, it is a function of the normal conscience and is an inbuilt part of our humanity. And *holding* people responsible for their actions is something that has to be done (by parents, by teachers, by the criminal law, and in all sorts of other social and personal ways) if the people in question do criminal or anti-social things, no matter that the things they do are determined. It is after all these particular people who have done the things in question, and who are therefore quite likely to do them again (unless free will really did exist, in which case there'd be no reason to think that past behaviour was any guide to future behaviour), and as a matter of practical necessity these particular people have to be identified as the "offenders" and taken in hand in one way or another. If the act of identifying them and taking them in hand equates to holding them responsible, then no one in their right mind would object to their being held responsible.

If once we accept the practical necessity of furthering good behaviour and defending ourselves against bad behaviour, even if the behaviour is determined, then the question whether determinism precludes moral responsibility becomes unimportant and hardly worth debating. It must surely be true that if a person's crime is determined, he or she does not *deserve* to be punished for it. But the italicised word needs to be emphasised. To my mind, the idea of the *deserved* punishment cannot be reconciled with determinism. If, to go back to my early formulation, a person acts as he does because he is the person he is, and he has not made himself the person he is, then the view that he deserves to be punished for what he does is not sustainable. But this doesn't mean that we should not take him in hand in some way or other, and it doesn't even mean that this taking in hand may not (for want of any better solution) involve locking him up in prison or treating him in some other way which he finds very unpleasant. The difference between inflicting this treatment because we need to do it, and inflicting it because he deserves to be punished, might well seem pretty theoretical to him. The theory is nonetheless important and can lead to constructive changes in the treatment, but that is something to look at later.

So where *does* all this leave "moral responsibility"? Moral responsibility, of course, is an abstract concept, and that's just the trouble. It isn't a thing whose existence in any given circumstances can be proved or disproved scientifically or in any other way. No doubt it can be defined – or rather, the conditions necessary for its existence can be defined – but there is no general agreement about the definition. The truth of the matter is that the concept of moral responsibility is unimportant in itself: it is important only because of what we take to be its implications – because of the consequences which seem to us to flow from it. In practice it is a sort of label which we stick on other people when we want to visit these consequences upon them. If you twisted my arm I'd have to say that moral responsibility is not compatible with determinism, because I can't see a sensible definition which would make it compatible, but this would not be to say anything of much practical importance; and if you came up with a definition which allowed you to take the opposite view I shouldn't want to argue very strongly because I don't think you'd be saying anything very important either. If (according to the definition being used) we are *not* morally responsible for what we do, this doesn't of itself prevent us from feeling bad if what we do is bad, and it doesn't preclude others from taking action against us if what we do is bad enough to be criminal or anti-social. Conversely if (according to some other definition) we *are* morally responsible for what we do, I should still want to assert, as I did before, that determinism cannot be reconciled with the idea of the deserved punishment. So let us give moral responsibility a respectful nod and then walk on: if we fall into conversation with it, we may never get away.

Just before we take our leave, however, one last point may be made. There is an unspoken assumption that there would be no problem about moral responsibility (or, at least, about its existence) if free will existed - that it is only the idea of determinism which casts doubt on it. But is this right? Even if free will did exist, there would still be a problem, surely, because it would then be difficult to identify the entity which had the moral responsibility. Burglar Bill is standing outside the empty house with his wholehearted desire to break in. This is the Burglar Bill we know and love. But suppose he did have free will, and suppose that, because of it, he walked away instead. His decision to do so would by definition be unmotivated, so it would be made by a Burglar Bill who was unknown to us, unknown to anyone else, unknown even to himself. Wouldn't it be quite difficult to attribute moral responsibility in these circumstances?

★ ★ ★ ★ ★

But are you still wondering about Kant and the noumenon? What Kant said was that total reality consists of two "worlds". The first is the world of our everyday experience – a world of material objects in space and time, a world of common sense and natural science, a world which can be labelled as the empirical world. But this world is mediated to us by our senses and it cannot, therefore, include anything which lies outside the possibility of our experience. So he thought there must be a second world which did contain such things, a world of things as they are "in themselves" rather than a world of things as they appear to us, and this other world he called the *noumenon*.

Kant accepted fully that the empirical world was one of cause and effect, one governed by scientific laws: in short, a world of determinism. But he thought that free will must nonetheless exist and that it must therefore be found in the noumenon – or rather, that it would never be *found* in the noumenon because the noumemon was forever closed to us, but that it was there all the same. But why did he think it must exist? He started from the perception that moral concepts – the idea that we ought to do this and ought not to do that – have practical significance for us. But, he said, they could not have this significance unless we possessed some degree of freedom of choice in our actions, because "*ought* implies *can*". Since, however, there could be no such freedom in the empirical world, part of us as human beings must lie outside that world: the part of us which exercises freedom of choice must be in the noumenal world. And because free will is exercised only in the noumenon it is incapable of any kind of explanation. It cannot be explained causally, it cannot be understood at all, and although, Kant says, we can know *that* it is, we can never know *what* it is. In this way Kant managed to reconcile his view that free will is incomprehensible with an insistence that it nonetheless exists. For him, indeed, it was an incomprehensible free will that exists.

But surely Kant's argument goes wrong almost at the start. His whole edifice is built on the assumption that morality could have no significance for us if there were no free will. But this just isn't so. Moral concepts have significance for us because, as I argued at the start of this chapter, evolution has built morality into us: it is an essential part of our evolved make-up as civilised beings. And we have built it into our civilisation in order to maintain and further that civilisation. Towards the end of Chapter 3, I asked some questions about the nature of free will: how could it work, what could it possibly *be*? And I ventured to declare them unanswerable and to dismiss free will as a nonsense. Kant, too, declares these questions unanswerable, but this does not trouble him because he consigns free will to the noumenon where all questions are unanswerable. The findings of neuroscience (Chapter 9), would suggest that Kant's free will, if it did exist, would have to be located somewhere in the physical brain, and perhaps there may be a joke here somewhere. Have you heard the one about the Kantian neurosurgeon who couldn't find parts of his patients' brains because they were in the noumenon?

Ted Honderich, the determinist philosopher who makes an occasional appearance in these pages, has made much shorter work than I have of Kant's approach to free will: it must, he says, be hopeless [32]. And perhaps I have spent a disproportionate amount of time on Kant's theory, but it is the kind of theory which philosophers propound, and Kant was, by common consent, a great philosopher.

18.

A determinist view
of oneself and others

The same determinist philosopher has expressed regret that his own belief in determinism prevents him from having a feeling he would like to have: that of "being [his] own man" [33]. Perhaps we can see what he means by this. It depends on how you picture yourself in the light of determinism. If you see yourself as nothing but a cog in the inexorable machine of causality, then maybe you don't feel like your own man, or your own woman. But you don't have to picture yourself like this. Try seeing yourself instead as a person with your own hereditary endowment, shaped and moulded by your own past life and experiences, and behaving as you do because you are that person. Does this make you feel better? And would you actually feel any more like your own man or woman if this were not so? Come to that, what on earth *would* you feel like if it were not so?

It's very doubtful whether an acceptance of determinism makes much difference to the way one feels about oneself. To judge from my own experience, it certainly doesn't make one feel less guilty about one's own behaviour. And why should it? I have to say again that an intellectual belief doesn't destroy feelings which proceed from a fundamental part of the personality (in this case, the conscience). It may perhaps alter slightly the nature of those feelings. Feelings of guilt about bad behaviour usually go hand in hand with the belief that one might have acted differently. The determinist knows this isn't so but is saddened instead by the light which the bad behaviour throws on the nature of his or her character. It comes to much the same thing. Speaking for myself, I do not feel in any way absolved from the regret and remorse which I feel about aspects of my life as I look back over it: determinism doesn't wash away these feelings. Nor, by the same token, would determinism destroy one's enjoyment of any success one might have achieved. If in some ways your life has been successful, you can still feel pleased: the fact you were caused to succeed – built to succeed, if you like, in a world built for you to succeed in – doesn't take much of the gilt off the gingerbread. And if in some important ways you have failed, the fact that you were built to fail in a world built for your failure is not much of a comfort.

And what about one's feelings for other people? One of the most important sources of resistance to determinism lies in the idea that it threatens to deprive us of emotional satisfactions. A great deal of what we are pleased to think about people, feel about them or do to them (either personally or through our social institutions) is thought to be justified only if free will exists. Jack and Jill have been seeing a lot of one another, and one day Jack tells Jill that he loves her. Later Jill meets an interfering girlfriend, who tells her that Jack's declaration of love was the product of determinism: a causal explanation for it lies in Jack's heredity and past environment. Jill is not happy with this and the friend asks why. "Well," says Jill, "I don't want it to be *determined*. I want it to be sort of ... *spontaneous*." The friend (and with a friend like this Jill needs no enemies) presses her further. Does she mean by "spontaneous" that she wants Jack's declaration of love to be plucked out of the air for no reason? No, of course she doesn't. She wants it to come from deep within Jack, to be a manifestation of Jack himself. But, persists the friend, how does she think Jack came to *be* himself: he wouldn't be himself, would he, but for the nature he was born with and the things that have happened to him? Jill chooses to pursue the conversation no further, but later still she sees Jack again and he renews his declaration, this time adding a proposal of marriage. Jill accepts the proposal enthusiastically and Jack says (because he is of a romantic turn of mind) that his whole life has been but a preparation for this blissful moment. Jill is delighted and says she feels just the same. Since we are both determinists, I have a certain affinity with Jill's girlfriend, so I could wish that she were a pleasant character, but evidently she is not, and if she were to overhear this exchange I am afraid she would greet it with a knowing and rather patronising smile.

There are many different feelings which people's behaviour may inspire in us, or ours may inspire in them, which – some might say – depend on free will and are inconsistent with determinism. One thinks of love, admiration, gratitude, anger, hate, contempt, resentment, hurt, forgiveness, and so on. If determinism means that you have to regard yourself and other people as products – products of the causality which has shaped us all – where does this leave such feelings? Can you really have them for a product of causality? Yes, of course you can. If acceptance of determinism destroyed them, it would destroy one's whole emotional life, and there is no possibility of that. No, these "products" are still the people for whom you may have all these feelings, and the people who may have them all for you. The feelings are not "invalidated". If we love someone, we love what they are, and we don't concern ourselves with how they got to be that way. A psychologist knows better than most people that our personality traits can be reduced to a scored assessment, a doctor that we are composed of flesh, blood, bone and intricate internal organs, a biologist that we contain ten times as many bacterial cells as we contain cells of our own, a chemist that we are made of the same dirty, elemental, inanimate stuff as the earth and the stars are made of, an undertaker that we are all dead bodies sooner or later, and a sub-atomic physicist that we consist almost entirely of empty space, but these pieces of knowledge do not affect their relationships with those who are close to them. And so it is with determinists, who may be prone intellectually to see people as tiny bits of the pattern in an unrolling carpet, but whose feelings for those they love or hate remain as strong as ever.

But there is more in it than this, as Jill's girlfriend knew and Jill herself may eventually have realised. To say that our feelings for others are real or meaningful only if free will exists is not just untrue: it is the opposite of the truth. Although our feelings for other people are necessarily evoked by their behaviour – by what they say and do – it is the people themselves for whom we have the feelings and we have them because they are the people their behaviour has shown them to be. And they don't somehow reinvent or recreate themselves before each bit of behaviour. The behaviour is an expression of their continuing natures, and if their natures did not have causal explanations they would not exist. Those who think they want free will to play a part in their personal relationships have not understood that it would make them unsustainable.

This is not meant to imply that an *acceptance* of determinism has no effect at all on these relationships. It is, after all, a bit of insight into the human condition, and all such insights tend to deepen our understanding and perhaps our sympathies. Look for a minute at two particular feelings included in the list above: anger and the feeling which sometimes overtakes it, forgiveness. If something makes you angry, it makes you angry, whether you are a determinist or not; and the fact that the behaviour which made you angry was determined does not dispel the anger. Professor Ted Honderich, the determinist philosopher mentioned at the start of this chapter, records in his autobiography [34], occasions on which he expressed great anger towards other people, and gives no hint that this may have been out of accord with his belief in determinism. And maybe it wasn't, because if people do bad things, anger (though it may not be deserved) is the natural reaction and its expression is a means by which they may be brought to mend their ways.

But forgiveness? As a law student I wrote an article about determinism in a students' magazine. In it I claimed that if you accept determinism you will find you can forgive anyone for almost anything. If there is someone still alive who read the article, I should like to apologise for this claim because it is very nearly complete nonsense. The aphorism, "*Comprendre c'est pardoner. Tout comprendre c'est tout pardoner*" [35], is attributed to Madame de Stael, but this seems to be wrong because what she actually wrote was, "*Tout comprendre rend tres indulgent*" [36]. Be that as it may, there is probably a lot of truth in whatever exactly was said by whoever it was that said it. But determinism doesn't, by itself, give you a detailed understanding of anyone's actions: it tells you only that their actions are capable in principle of being understood. And I have to say yet again that strong feelings are not to be dispelled or fundamentally changed by an intellectual concept. It's true, too, that hurtful acts throw light on the character of the person who does them, and this is none the less so − actually, it is *only* so − because the acts were determined; and there's nothing in determinism which requires or enables you to like people who show themselves to be dislikeable, however causally determined their dislikeability may be. I should want nonetheless to suggest that there was a tiny grain of truth in the claim in the article. Acceptance of determinism does bring with it the realisation that people's bad behaviour, though it is most certainly a *fault in them*, is not their fault; and if you couple this with the realisation that their behaviour may do harm to them as well as to you and others, then forgiveness may be a little bit easier.

Philosophers, it seems to me, don't always recognise the importance of emotion as a motivating force, and its primacy over reason, so I was glad to find, after I had completed what I thought would be the final version of this chapter, that a similar approach had been taken by the philosopher, Sir Peter Strawson, in an influential essay written in 1962 called *Freedom and Resentment* [37]. Although he thought that determinism was true and that free will was incoherent, he understood and emphasised the primacy of human feeling and human interaction. (He referred in passing to psychoanalysis, and perhaps a knowledge of this subject may have played a part in his perception.) Referring to such emotions as gratitude, resentment, "reciprocated adult loves" and "essentially personal antagonisms", he said:

> The human commitment to participation in ordinary inter-personal relationships is, I think, too thoroughgoing and deeply rooted for us to take seriously the thought that a general theoretical conviction [of the truth of determinism] might so change our world that, in it, there were no longer any such things as inter-personal relationships as we normally understand them ...

Amen to that. Later he says that this view may be thought to leave "the real question unanswered" – this question being "... about what it would be rational to do if determinism were true, a question about the rational justification of ordinary inter-personal attitudes in general." In response to this question, my own urge is to hark back to my Chapter 15 and assert simply that there is no such thing as a rational justification for emotion. What *rational* justification could there be for wanting to stay alive, for wanting to have children, for wanting to give and receive love, or indeed for wanting to preserve the human race? None of these desires is rational because emotions are not rational, and we are not governed by reason but by emotion.

Despite the fact (an obvious one, it seems to me) that "we cannot ... seriously envisage ourselves adopting a thoroughgoing objectivity of attitude to others as a result of theoretical conviction of the truth of determinism", Sir Peter Strawson emphasises nonetheless that it is possible, sometimes and for particular purposes, to step back from our reactive attitude and to bring some objectivity to bear. For myself, I believe strongly that, in considering our feelings for other people, there's an important distinction to be drawn between the people we know – who include our families and friends and all those with whom we come into personal contact – and the rest. The rest consist of people we don't know, people in general or particular groups of people. Inasmuch as we may be able to see these other people more objectively, it is in relation to them that an acceptance of determinism may make a real difference to our feelings, or at least to our approach, because it is in relation to them that emotion is less pressing and reason more easily engaged. The best and strongest example of this, and its greatest test, lies in the field of crime and punishment, and Part V of this book is concerned with that subject.

19.

Why doesn't free will self-destruct?

All right, you may say, if real free will really is so nonsensical, why has belief in it persisted for so long? Why, despite its undoubted emotional attractions, has its invalidity not forced itself upon us? Why hasn't it *shown* itself to be invalid? The answer to that question may provide a bridge between this part of the book and the next.

It is just possible that our civilisation is edging its way very gradually towards an implicit rejection of free will. Already we are ambivalent about it, behaving for much of the time as if doesn't exist. A limited version of it makes no more sense than a full one. Medical, psychological and scientific studies of human behaviour have no room for it, and yet we accept their findings. Respectable neuroscientists deny its existence. And although (more of this later) our criminal law is founded on free will, the few constructive elements in our penal system are geared to reform, not retribution. So are we coming, little by little, to accept determinism unawares?

Perhaps I should be mildly encouraged by the fairy story of *The Emperor's New Clothes*. You will remember that two weavers offered to make the Emperor a magnificent suit of clothes from cloth which they would weave. The cloth would be beautifully coloured, exquisitely patterned and, above all, extraordinarily fine – so fine, they said, that stupid people might not be able to see it at all. Everyone to whom the cloth was later shown, including the Emperor himself, praised it highly because they didn't want to be thought stupid, and when it was made into clothes for the Emperor he wore them proudly in a procession. All the onlookers joined in admiring them until one small child pointed out that the Emperor was naked: the weavers were swindlers and the clothes did not exist. If everyone had gone on believing in the existence of the clothes, I wonder how the child would have set out to justify his assertion. But in fact they didn't: once the child had spoken, the people whispered among themselves and decided that he was right.

It is true nonetheless that our idea of free will, vague, amorphous and ultimately incoherent as it may be, is still so much a part of our culture that most of us see everything around us through (as it were) free-will-coloured spectacles. We think we discern the workings of free will in our world, just as religious people think they discern the workings of God. And this vision is self-validating and self-perpetuating, because the more we see the world in this way the more reason we think we have to believe that it really is this way. And we aren't going to take off the spectacles because we don't know we're wearing them.

Suppose that, like Ted Honderich, the determinist philosopher mentioned in the last chapter and in other parts of this book, we get very angry with someone who has done us a bad turn and tear them off a strip. If we believe in free will, we think we are justified in this because the someone has done us the bad turn in exercise of their free will, and so is to blame for doing it and therefore deserves our wrath and condemnation; and if the someone then mends their ways, we take this to show that they do indeed have free will because they must have exercised it in order to bring about the change. But there is an alternative version of these events and if we removed our spectacles we should see it: that the someone didn't really deserve our anger because they were "programmed" by past circumstances to do what they did, but that our anger did nonetheless serve a useful purpose, not because it prompted them to modify their future behaviour through an exercise of free will, but because it inserted something new into the chain of causation which would determine that behaviour.

This point is worth amplifying. Despite determinism (or rather, because of determinism) people's future thoughts, feelings and actions may be changed by events. Just as determinism does not preclude the possibility that people may change themselves if they want to change, so it does not preclude the possibility that they may be changed by the influences which are brought to bear upon them. Angry condemnation of bad behaviour which brings about better behaviour may be justified and even helpful to the person at whom it is directed. Usually, however, behaviour can be modified only by means which are more constructive and perhaps less simple. What kind of a something – an admonition, a penalty, a bit of praise, a long discussion, a better education, a training course, a job, a helping hand, a course of psychotherapy – needs to be pushed into the causal chain in order to achieve the desirable result? It must be such that, taken in conjunction with all the other motivations in the matrix of the subject's personality, it is enough to do the job. Sometimes there is simply nothing which will do the job. Means may exist to persuade someone not to take their first dose of heroin, or perhaps even their second, but there may be no means at all to persuade them not to take their hundredth or their thousandth.

A book concerned with the neuroscientific approach to free will and determinism, dealt with in Chapter 9, upset one of its reviewers[38]. The book recorded the consensus among neuroscientists that free will doesn't exist and quoted the words of one of them, Dr. Steven Pinker, who had described it as "a fictional construction". This made the reviewer rather cross: "Why isn't Pinker a passionate opponent of any punishment for crime, in that case? You might as well discipline a great white shark for swallowing a surfer." I think the reviewer is falling victim to a fallacy here. Perhaps it is the idea that determinism means you cannot change and cannot be changed and, in particular, that punishment cannot change you. This may be so for the great white shark, but it isn't necessarily so for human beings. Punishment does serve a purpose in a deterministic world - and does so precisely because the world is deterministic. It has at least the potential to modify human behaviour. The threat of future punishment, the memory of past punishment, the fear of more punishment for further misbehaviour ... all these things operate for human beings by pushing another determinant into the causal chain.

This determinant may or may not be potent enough, taken in the context of the offender's whole personality, to affect the outcome, and it is certainly true that punishment by itself is not a very effective way to change criminal behaviour. The criminal justice system is coming increasingly to recognise this, and to discover that more constructive remedies for crime produce better results, but society has to defend itself somehow against those who would disrupt it and no determinist could sensibly deny that punishment has some effect and may (for want of anything better) sometimes be justifiable. If someone had managed to persuade Kant that there was no noumenon or that, if there was, it didn't contain free will, I can't help thinking that he would still have felt forced to justify punishment on this ground.

But we need to draw a distinction between the kind of punishment which serves a useful purpose and the kind which is inflicted simply to cause physical or emotional hurt to the offender. Punishment of the former kind is *deterrent* punishment: punishment designed simply to deter the offender from future crime, and perhaps to deter other potential offenders from committing crimes of their own. But there is also punishment of the latter kind - punishment designed as *retribution*. Retributory punishment, in so far as it goes beyond deterrent punishment, as usually it does, really is unjustifiable in the light of determinism, but it is to this kind of punishment that most of us cling very tenaciously. We cling to it, as I shall try to explain in more detail in later chapters, not because it serves any useful purpose, but because it gives us emotional satisfaction. We value the emotional catharsis which it provides and, because it seems to rest upon the idea of free will, we cling to that as well. We really feel the need to see "wickedness" in people and to punish them because of it – and I think we feel this need, not just because of what they actually do, but because we want somehow to challenge, purge or destroy the wickedness which they embody and display. The mechanisms involved are exactly the same as those which led us, in earlier centuries, to hang and burn witches. And, in a very real sense, we're still doing this and most of us don't want to stop.

PART V

DETERMINISM, CRIME AND PUNISHMENT

PART IV

DETERMINISM, CRIME AND PUNISHMENT

20.

The real causes of crime

From a determinist point of view all crime, like every other human activity, has a causal explanation, and particular crimes committed by particular individuals are the result of long and complex chains of causality affecting those individuals. Things have gone "wrong" on the journey which takes them from conception to adult life. Some years ago Dr Edward Glover, a psychiatrist who was also one of the second generation of psychoanalysts, said [39], "Crime is part of the price paid for the domestication of a naturally wild animal."

You don't have to accept psychoanalytic theory in order to think that this is pretty accurate. The multifarious and ingenious ways in which great numbers of people inflict physical, mental or other harm on one another, not just without qualms but with enjoyment, must lend some credibility to it. And if it is accurate, then the things that go wrong may not be things which turn the individual towards crime so much as things which fail to turn him or her away from it – failures, you could say, in a civilising or domesticating process which all of us have to negotiate successfully, with the loving help of our parents or other adults, if we are to become useful and law-abiding citizens. But the point to emphasise is that the journey which we take is a complicated and difficult one: things can go wrong in many different ways, at many different stages, to many different degrees and with many different results.

When New Labour devised its slogan, "Tough on crime, and tough on the causes of crime", what kind of causes did it plan to be tough on? Presumably things like poverty, bad housing, unemployment, run-down estates, poor education, perhaps poor parenting in those cases in which it could be discovered and dealt with ... These are the sort of things which a government might in theory be able to tackle. But are they really the causes of crime? One of the striking facts about governments is that, powerful as they are, the instruments at their disposal are very blunt. All the ills mentioned above must certainly play some part - if usually an indirect part - in producing individual criminals, and crime as a whole would most certainly fall dramatically if, by some miracle, they could all be eliminated, but to call them the causes of crime is seriously misleading.

Still longer ago another doctor described tuberculosis of the lung as the end of a song sung to a child in its cradle [40]. Whether or not this was (or still is) true of tuberculosis, it is certainly true of crime and other anti-social behaviour. And of course the song starts well before the child gets into the cradle, because inborn characteristics play a big part in the determining process. Nature and nurture combine, the one reacting with the other. Cruelty and misfortune may turn one child (a naturally introverted one) into an emotional cripple and another (an extraverted child) into a habitual criminal. If Laplace's Demon could write, and tried to give a written explanation of the criminality of an individual criminal (or, for that matter, the entrepreneurial skill of an individual business tycoon, or the saintliness of an individual saint), goodness knows how long the explanation would be. It would be the story of the multi-million events in their developing lives and their effects, the multi-million events in their developing brains. Words like "poverty" and "bad housing" don't begin to do the job.

Because the causes of crime tend to be expressed in these simple terms, and there is no general understanding of the real complexity of causation, people tend to reject out of hand the very idea that

116

crime *has* causes. To say that it is caused by bad housing, poverty, lack of work, bad schooling, poor physical environment, unhappy childhood, or by some other easily-expressed factor, is to invite the retort that there are people who suffer these particular deprivations and yet turn into law-abiding citizens (which is perfectly true), with the strong implication that these things don't really cause crime at all because it must be open to those who suffer them to exercise their free will, shrug them off and get on with their lives as if nothing had happened. The story is told of a boys' adventure serial featuring a hero called Jack. At the end of one episode Jack found himself in an appalling situation, tied hand and foot and trapped so securely that no one could see how he could possibly extricate himself. Readers awaited the next episode with trepidation, but when it came out it began with the words, "With one bound Jack was free ...". Burglar Bill isn't going to free himself from crime with one bound, and neither is any other criminal. (Perhaps we may wonder whether the behaviour of the Roman Catholic Church, in taking no action against its paedophile priests except to reprimand them and transfer them to other parishes, has been due partly to a naïve belief that free will really does have a transformative power of this kind.)

It is absolutely true that different people may emerge with different propensities from backgrounds which, if you describe them broadly, look much the same; but this is only because the backgrounds are described much too broadly and the people subjected to them really are different people - people with different genetic capacities to cope with, and react to, the events which befall them. Not long ago a well known historian said: "There were plenty of people in upper Austria who had much the same potty training as Adolf Hitler, but who did not go on to unleash a war that killed over 50 million people." He was commenting on a suggestion that Hitler's character was affected for the worse by his early experiences of toilet training. The suggestion must have come from someone with psychoanalytical leanings who had seized upon some of Freud's ideas about anal aggression. The moral must be, *Don't oversimplify*: if you do, you will invite superficially clever but actually rather shallow retorts like this.

These points were strikingly illustrated not long ago in a newspaper article. A child had been drugged and abducted, and her mother and uncle were found guilty of carrying out the abduction. Their plan was to let some time elapse and then pretend to have found the child and go on to collect the reward money. *The Times* of 5 December 2008 carried a leading article about the case. It started by conceding that the offenders were "stupid" and "inadequate"; that they lived on a "grim estate" where "relentlessly depressing stories of dirt and depression and chaotic lives strike hard"; and that the mother was living "without work, or the prospect of work". But then followed the predictable counter-argument: "There are many people who … lack the standard intellectual tools, yet still are able to make the basic distinction between right and wrong …. There are also many people who live in poverty and in grim estates, yet still try their best to care for their children and live decent lives". And finally came the equally predictable and rather triumphant conclusion that, although "seeking for an explanation to [*sic*] inexplicable acts of evil is understandable … the crimes of [the two defendants] are ultimately theirs, and theirs alone". How true. And it is true, too, that the complex chains of causality which *really* determined their crimes were also theirs and theirs alone. Those who wish to characterise these crimes as "acts of evil" are free to do so, but can we really go on believing that such acts are in principle "inexplicable"?

What might be called the "broad description syndrome" sometimes leads even to a complete misunderstanding of what those who believe that crime has causes are really trying to say. Members of the general public just can't imagine how these broadly-described factors can be said to lead inevitably to crime – and of course their scepticism is fully justified because they don't. Such people may, for example, have had rotten childhoods themselves, but this hasn't turned them into criminals and they don't see why (or how) backgrounds like theirs would have that effect on anyone else. As a result, they interpret references to these broad causal factors as being in some sense mere "excuses" or pleas for a sort of compensatory leniency. They think the suggestion is that, because criminals have experienced one or more of these deprivations, they should be punished less severely or not punished at all – on the basis, presumably, that they've suffered enough already. Any ideas of this kind rest, of course, on a complete misunderstanding of the determinist position.

On 3 January 2010 the *Observer* carried a story about a special school for children traumatised by violence in their homes. Lucy, aged nine, had been neglected from birth: she had been both physically and sexually abused and she had seen her mother beat her older sister to death. So when Lucy played with her dolls she acted out her experiences of violence and invented stories in which the dolls were tortured and murdered. No doubt she was trying to objectify and come to terms with what had happened to her. Let us hope that the special school manages to undo some of the harm she has suffered. But our hopes should not be raised too high: there is strong evidence that this kind of severe abuse can actually damage a child's brain, affecting its normal development. And if the school cannot repair the damage and she acts out these terrible early experiences in the form of crime when she grows up, the experiences won't be "excuses" which qualify her for "leniency": they will be purely and simply the determinants of the crimes she commits. And if you were born with the same heredity as Lucy, and subjected to exactly the same experiences – if all your life had been exactly the same as all of hers – you would behave in the same way. Wouldn't you?

So what is the determinist position? Simply that criminals and their criminal conduct are produced by complex chains of causality which cannot be broadly or simply described but which are capable, if only in principle, of being analysed and understood. The important question of course is, what follows from this? What implications does it have for our attitude towards criminals and other anti-social people? These are the questions I want now to explore, but I should preface the exploration by admitting at once that it doesn't *necessarily* have any implications at all. It's a trite philosophical saying that you can't get an "ought" from an "is": that a factual state of affairs, however clearly established, doesn't of itself entail any moral consequences. In the middle of the twentieth century the then Lord Chief Justice, Lord Goddard, told the Royal Commission on Capital Punishment that a convicted murderer whom he considered to be quite clearly insane should nonetheless be hanged. His insanity was, as the judge put it, "one of the reasons why he should be out of the way". You may think that the idea of hanging an insane man abhorrent (and so do I), but the fact that he is insane does not entail the *logical* consequence that he should not be hanged, because his insanity is a matter of fact and the way we treat him is a matter of morality. If our view of morality, like that of Lord Goddard, does not conflict with our hanging him, that's that.

And if our view of morality allows us to go on treating criminals as if they had free will and created their own criminality, that's that too. Determinists can do no more than set out their stall – tell it like they think it is – and then leave other people, if they are convinced, to decide upon the consequences according to their own moral standards.

21.

The incoherent aims of sentencing

The purposes to be served in sentencing convicted offenders are now declared for the first time in an Act of Parliament: according to section 142 of the Criminal Justice Act 2003, they are (in the case of adults):

(a) the punishment of offenders,
(b) the reduction of crime (including its reduction by deterrence),
(c) the reform and rehabilitation of offenders,
(d) the protection of the public, and
(e) the making of reparation by offenders to persons affected by their offences.

For many years, books about criminology and the penal system listed these same aims, but all of them used to be set out under the general heading of "Punishment". Clearly it is better (and must be reckoned as some small progress towards rationality) that only one of them is now described in this way. But in order to distinguish it from the others, that one used to be listed in the books as "Retribution", and this, of course, is what it still is. The aim of "punishment", as listed in the 2003 Act, is wholly retributive. It enshrines the idea that the offender should be made to suffer simply and solely because he or she has made others suffer.

And this aim - punishment, in the sense of retributive punishment - is the odd one out. All the other aims are at least positive, designed to serve some useful purpose, but this one, though its fulfilment may certainly give satisfaction to the public, does no actual good to anyone. It certainly does no good to the offender. Pursuit of the other aims in the list would allow the court to do all that can be done to turn the offender away from crime. That purpose could still be served, equally well if not better, were "punishment" to be struck out of the list altogether. The aim of retributive punishment as such is therefore, from a utilitarian point of view, surplus to requirements. And this aim is the odd one out in another respect, too, because it is the only one which depends for its justification on the existence of free will and is inconsistent with determinism. Acceptance of determinism doesn't of itself make any of the other aims look wrong or unattainable: in so far as their object is to change behaviour, there is nothing in determinism which says it can't be changed by these means. But determinism really *is* inconsistent with the idea that punishment is *deserved* and this is the essence of retribution.

And yet, in this modern statutory list of sentencing aims, retributive punishment heads all the rest, and it does so because it dominates all the rest − in reality, in the public mind and in the minds of successive Home Secretaries, if not in the aspirations of penologists. If it is not a useful thing, why is it still considered so important? The reason is, as I've already suggested, that the public finds it satisfying and sets a great deal of store by it. But that is for the next chapter. This one sets out to illustrate how all-important the idea of retribution really is and the way in which our desire to hang on to it leads to illogicalities and impossible distinctions.

My illustration has to do with the ways in which the penal system deals with the different mental states which lead someone to commit murder. Let's start with the mental condition which is at the opposite end of the scale from "normality": that's to say, insanity within the *M'Naghten Rules*. These rules were laid down in the mid-nineteenth century at a time when the mandatory sentence for murder was death by hanging. They take their name from Daniel M'Naghten who, in 1843, intending to shoot Sir Robert Peel, the Prime Minister, shot his secretary instead. He was acquitted of murder because he was insane and was committed to a mental institution. Queen Victoria, who had herself been the subject of assassination attempts, was not amused by this outcome because it seemed to her unduly lenient and she had the matter referred to the House of Lords. As a result, the judges of the common law courts were asked to formulate a legal test of insanity and they produced the *M'Naghten Rules*. Under the Rules, the legal test is that "the accused was labouring under such a defect of reason, from disease of the mind, as not to know the nature and quality of the act he was doing; or, if he did know it, that he did not know he was doing what was wrong." If this is proved, the accused will be found "not guilty by reason of insanity" and will normally be confined in a secure mental hospital. To him or her, this outcome may seem very much like punishment but, although no one would say it was "deserved", no one with any sense would quarrel with it.

Our whole penal system – the rules about the way in which crime is to be viewed and criminals are to be treated – is based very firmly on the idea of free will, but *M'Naghten* insanity is a complete defence because it is taken completely to negate free will. In relation to this particular defence, therefore, all is harmony between proponents of free will, who are in charge of the system, and determinists. But this harmony, as we shall see, is not going to last.

Psychiatrists and others came increasingly to dislike the *M'Naghten Rules*, thinking them narrow and outmoded, and by section 2 of the Homicide Act 1957 Parliament created the *partial* defence of "diminished responsibility". This was available when the accused was suffering, not from insanity within the Rules, but from "such abnormality of mind ... as substantially impaired his mental

123

responsibility ...". Diminished responsibility leads to an accused being convicted, not of murder, but of the lesser crime of manslaughter. Nowadays murder attracts a mandatory sentence of life imprisonment, so a manslaughter conviction may result in a less severe sentence, although in practice it often results in life imprisonment or a hospital order.

Does this partial defence stand up to examination, even from a traditionally free will point of view? It applies when the abnormality "impairs" the accused's "mental responsibility". What meaning can you attach to this idea? If the abnormality impairs the accused's mental responsibility for the killing, this must necessarily be because it impairs his or her ability to refrain from it. Yet because this ability is only "impaired", it must follow that *some* ability is thought to remain. It must follow also that the remaining ability is thought sufficient to *enable* the accused to refrain: otherwise why should there be any conviction at all? But if that is so, why should there not be a conviction for murder plain and simple?

The Homicide Act definition of diminished responsibility has now been replaced by section 52 of the Coroners and Justice Act 2009. "Abnormality of mind" becomes "abnormality of mental functioning [arising] from a recognised medical condition". This abnormality must have "substantially impaired [the accused's] ability" to understand the nature of his or her conduct, to form a rational judgment or to exercise self-control. So the idea of "impairment" is carried over from the old definition to the new, where it gives rise to the same conceptual difficulties. But in the 2009 Act there is something new. The abnormality must also "provide an explanation" for the accused's behaviour in doing the killing, and this means that it "causes, or is a significant contributory factor in causing" that behaviour. No doubt this provision is meant to ensure that the abnormality is *relevant*: if it consisted *solely* in an inability to tell a hawk from a handsaw, it would be no defence to a killing which involved no hawks or handsaws. But the result is remarkable: the accused may actually be *caused* to kill by an abnormality arising from a recognised medical condition and *still* be convicted of the crime of manslaughter.

The difficulties and contradictions which we see here, and shall see again later in this chapter, spring from an attempt to reconcile two things. On the one hand, there is the pressing need to take some account of modern knowledge about the causal effect which mental illness has on crime even if the illness falls short of the outdated formula in the *M'Naghten Rules*. On the other is the equally pressing need not to do this by calling into question the general principle of culpability and the deserved punishment. So we end up with the idea of *impaired* responsibility (in the 1957 Act), or *impaired* ability (in the 2009 Act), leading to *impaired* culpability. Ultimately this partial defence of diminished responsibility represents a compromise between free will and determinism. The result is reminiscent of the "little bit of free will in there somewhere" which made its appearance in Chapter 14 and it is equally unworkable because it poses the same difficulties.

The compromise reached is nonetheless one which most members of the public find acceptable because they can see that the kind of offender who successfully pleads this partial defence should be treated differently from an ordinary murderer and they will go along with a little bit of "leniency" provided that their core belief in free will and wickedness is not challenged. They accept that, if an accused is to be classed as fully wicked, he or she must be free of insanity or substantial mental abnormality. If these things are part of the causal chain which leads the offender to the crime, they will have some "sympathy" for him or her, but if a causal chain, however ineluctable, does not incorporate these particular features, they will normally have none. I say "normally" because every so often some other bit of the causal chain will catch the public imagination and excite sympathy. Publicity was given not long ago to the number of violent crimes committed by soldiers affected by their service in Iraq and Afghanistan and, because this particular link in the causal chain engaged public sympathy, there were calls for "comprehensive psychological treatment" to be made available to these potential offenders. (Some hope.) But the fact that crimes are *always* the result of a causal chain, whether or not it includes elements which happen to attract sympathy or understanding, is not recognised or accepted. In general we prefer to follow *The Times*, in its leading article quoted in the last chapter, and see them as "inexplicable acts of evil".

Let's press on a little further with our illustration. The next stage must be prefaced by an explanation. The sentence which convicted murderers actually serve is a little more flexible than it looks. Although hanging was once the mandatory sentence, individual murderers could still be reprieved. And although the mandatory sentence is now life imprisonment, this is an "indeterminate" sentence and doesn't necessarily mean that the offender never gets out of gaol alive. He or she may be released on "licence" (so that recall is possible) if and when the Parole Board considers it safe, but the Parole Board doesn't normally come into the picture until the offender has served a minimum term fixed by the judge at the trial. In the Criminal Justice Act 2003, Schedule 21, Parliament laid down detailed guidelines for the judge to apply in fixing this minimum term. They are far too long to be set out here, but anyone who does plough through them will gain a clear insight into the attitudes which Parliament, on behalf of society, brings to bear, at the beginning of the 21st century, on criminal motivation and the aims of sentencing.

The guidelines take the form of "starting points" which the judge is to apply to different categories of murder grouped together according to their "seriousness". Free will makes a very clear appearance at this point because the seriousness of an offence is tied explicitly, by section 143 of the Act, to "the offender's culpability". Broadly, in the case of offenders aged 21 or more, there are three categories: murders where the starting point is to be "a whole life order" (so that the Parole Board never gets a look-in at all unless the Secretary of State chooses to ask for their advice, which may or may not be accepted); murders where the starting point is 30 years; and the rest, where the starting point is 15 years. Having fixed the starting point, the judge must then decide whether to increase or reduce it in the light of "aggravating factors" and "mitigating factors" which are also set out in detail. Two particular points may form part of our illustration.

The first is another reference to mental illness. If the offender suffered from a mental disorder or disability which wasn't bad enough to fall within the *M'Naghten Rules* and wasn't bad enough to amount to diminished responsibility, but which nonetheless "lowered his degree of culpability", this is a mitigating factor. So now we have four mental states which courts are supposed to be able to distinguish: *M'Naghten* insanity, the abnormality required for diminished responsibility, the lesser disorder which amounts to a mitigating factor, and the mental state which for want of a better word must be described as normal. These artificial gradations of culpability are dictated by the need to preserve the idea of free will (which is supposed to exist in differing percentages), and they make about as much sense as the theological debate about the number of angels who can dance on the head of a pin.

The second point is this. Among the crimes for which the starting point is "whole life" we find "the murder of a child involving the abduction of the child or sexual or sadistic motivation". But we also find that if the child's murder does not involve any of these things, the starting point is not even 30 years but 15 years. What is there in the list of "aims" set out at the start of this chapter which justifies the much greater severity with which the first case is treated? We search in vain for any such justification in aims (b), (c), (d) and (e). So of course we are left with aim (a), punishment in the sense of retribution, and we have once again to recognise the all-important nature of this aim. It is the only aim which can justify the different treatment of the two child murderers.

And incidentally, what exactly is it about "sexual or sadistic motivation" which makes the murder more "serious" than it would otherwise be? Perhaps the answer is that the child's death may then be especially terrifying or especially painful or both – unimaginably so, in fact? Well, no, it isn't, because sexual or sadistic murder doesn't necessarily involve these things, and they are in any case dealt with separately among the "aggravating factors", where we find "mental or physical suffering inflicted on the victim before death". So sexual or sadistic motivation is not singled out in the "starting points" because it aggravates the victim's suffering: it is singled out because the mere possession of this motivation is thought to make the murderer more wicked, culpable, blameworthy, deserving of retributive punishment. (It's worth noting that "sexual and sadistic conduct" in relation to *any* murder lifts it straight out of the 15 year category and into the 30 year one.) Through the eyes of the judge, society looks into the mind of the murderer, finds evil there, and adds further punishment because of it. The fact that the impulse to sadistic or sexual murder represents a gross distortion of the human personality, which can come about only through a miserable genetic inheritance or the most unfavourable environmental influences, is not thought relevant. Here as elsewhere, wickedness is all.

In a case in 2009 the murderer had removed some flesh from the dead body of his victim, cooked it and tried to eat it before spitting it out. Although there was nothing in the guidelines to lift this case out of the 15 year category and into the 30 year one, the judge had nonetheless imposed a 30 year minimum term, and the Court of Appeal supported him. The Lord Chief Justice said that although the desecration of the body was "not a feature expressly identified in Schedule 21, it was … a profoundly significant feature of seriousness". The additional term of 15 years' imprisonment (the difference between a minimum term of 15 years and one of 30) which this offender has to serve before the Parole Board can consider his case is retributive punishment pure and simple.

So when it comes to sexual, sadistic or perverted feelings, it seems that we have reached a sticking point. A personality which harbours these feelings is not one which you or I would care to be saddled with and is certainly not one with which we would willingly saddle ourselves. A visitor from Mars, untutored in our society's approach to crime, might even think that possession of these feelings, though they would most certainly require society to be protected from their possessor while they lasted, might amount to a disorder which reduced culpability by one of the many degrees by which, apparently, it can be reduced. But no: this particular kind of disorder must go to increase culpability, not to reduce it. Instinctively we may feel inclined to agree with this view, but it makes no *sense* at all. And there is an interesting paradox here: criminals of the kind we have been talking about are often labelled by the popular press as "sick", but this word is not to be taken as a description of the disordered personalities which they certainly possess, still less as a factor which reduces their culpability, but rather as a term of abuse and condemnation.

The preoccupation of this chapter with mental abnormality must not be misunderstood. My purpose is not to suggest that the law should enlarge the category of offenders to whom it accords leniency on the ground of abnormality, and correspondingly reduce the category of "normal" offenders whom it treats as ripe for retributive punishment. My purpose is rather to suggest that our attempt to create and sustain these two categories is dictated by a wish to preserve the idea of free will in the face of the findings of the behavioural sciences; and that this wish has pushed us into creating anomalies, refinements and distinctions which go only to show that, in the end, the wish itself cannot be fulfilled. Of *course* offenders differ from one another in their mental states, doing so to an almost infinite degree, and these differences should be reflected in the way in which they are treated by the penal system, but there are causal explanations for the crimes of all of them, free will affects none of them, and *retributive* punishment is not something which any of them deserves or from which any would benefit.

The next chapter tries to give a fuller answer to the question why the public in general clings so tenaciously to retribution and its inseparable companion, free will.

22.

Society's need for retribution

The purpose of the last chapter was to show two things in particular. First, that out of all the officially declared aims of sentencing, punishment (punishment, that is, which has no object other than retribution) was alone in serving no useful purpose. And second, that it does nonetheless dominate society's approach to crime, as expressed in the penal system, where it creates confused and untenable distinctions. From a rational point of view, this seems strange. From an emotional one, however, it is not hard to understand.

The key lies in the fact that we are none of us born "good". The psychiatrist and psychoanalyst who said that crime is part of the price paid for the domestication of a naturally wild animal made his comment in a talk to a group of women magistrates. In another part of the same talk he went on to amplify it [41]:

> "[T]he perfectly normal infant is almost completely egocentric, greedy, dirty, violent in temper, destructive in habit, profoundly sexual in purpose, aggrandising in attitude, devoid of all but the most primitive reality sense, without conscience or moral feeling, whose attitude to society (as represented by the family) is opportunist, inconsiderate, domineering and sadistic.... In fact, judged by adult social standards, the normal baby is for all practical purposes a born criminal."

Some might think that this is putting it a bit high. After the talk the lady who chaired the meeting said, "But, doctor the dear babies!

How could you say such awful things about them?" Babies *are* lovable, but these words are pretty accurate nonetheless. If an adult, in an adult situation and armed with an adult's knowledge, intelligence and strength, and perhaps with an adult's weapons, behaved in the way a baby behaves, we shouldn't hesitate to describe him or her in this sort of way. Another psychiatrist expressed the same point more shortly [42]: "The criminal ... acts as a child would act, if it only could."

So if we are to reach adulthood as law-abiding and useful members of society, we have a lot of "bad", uncivilised tendencies to overcome. In favourable circumstances we manage the journey more or less successfully. But what happens to the bad tendencies? They don't just vanish into thin air: they are part of our make-up as human beings – part of the aggressive endowment which has brought us to the top of the evolutionary tree – and we still harbour them, although we don't act upon them save in the most exceptional circumstances and, for the most part, we don't acknowledge their existence. There is more in what W.B. Yeats called "the foul rag and bone shop of the heart" than we want to know about, and it isn't just inert stuff like rags and bones. And the fact that all its members have criminal tendencies which they are forbidden to express and choose not to recognise has a profound effect on the attitudes which society brings to bear upon those whose journey to adulthood has been less successful and who express these same tendencies in the form of criminal acts.

In 1602 a woman was brought before a court and accused of witchcraft. Evidence was given that she was mentally ill, but the judge would have none of it. According to a contemporary report [43] he "... spake to the Jewry [jury] as followeth, The Land is full of witches; they abounde in all places; I have hanged five or sixe and twenty of them ..." Nowadays we know that there are no such things as witches, so what the judge thought he had found in the women whom he boasted of having hanged – communion with the devil, an all-consuming desire to do harm for its own sake and magical powers to do it – weren't really there at all. So where did the perception of these things come from? It came, of course, from within the judge. The evil which he saw in them was the evil which, for all that it inhabited him, he didn't see in himself. To use a useful bit of psychological jargon, he projected it into them. (Projection has been defined [44] as "the tendency to attribute to other persons emotions, ideas, or attitudes which they do not in fact possess, but which take origin within ourselves.")

It is this mechanism of projection which allowed people long ago to make use of scapegoats. Originally the scapegoat was a real goat, and people got rid of their sins by putting them into it and then driving it into the wilderness. We no longer use goats for this purpose, but we do use other people, and criminals make very useful scapegoats. The criminal brings us an outlet for our own unacknowledged criminality because we can identify with him or her and become criminals ourselves by proxy. But we gain further relief when we punish the criminal because the act of punishment not only expresses our own destructive wishes but allows us to feel that we are doing so for the sake of righteousness. If we have indeed projected our bad feelings into the criminal, then those feelings are punished in him or her without the need for any suffering on our part, and we end up feeling good in more ways than one. We also feel at some level that punishment, by defending society against the criminal, defends us against our own criminality. So we can turn the criminal metaphorically into the wilderness and tell ourselves that he or she deserves to go and will be all the better for going; and we can bolster up our own conscious sense of virtue by doing so.

Crime is very important to us. Not only are the newspapers full of real crime, but fictional crime, much of it violent, looms large in our lives as well – in films, in theatre, television and radio plays, in detective stories and thrillers. But we don't hear very much about crime as a product of causality or about the ways in which it might be prevented: these things don't enter into the game we're playing – the game of scapegoats – because the object of this game is to avoid looking below the surface of things. The players of this game must align themselves with *The Times* in its leading article and see crimes as "acts of evil" which are "inexplicable". They want vicariously to be bad, to be punished for being bad, and then to be made good again ... all without the need to suffer any real pain or danger or even to move out of their armchairs. But they don't want to *know* that they are doing this. They don't want to know about the badness in themselves; and if they did, the game would become pointless and unnecessary.

Doesn't envy come into this situation, too? There is, surely, a part of us which resents the fact that civilisation has deprived us of our instinctive ways of behaving. In a real sense, the civilising process has made us suffer. The criminal is one who seems to have escaped this curbing and stultifying process, and we feel some unacknowledged envy because, in doing so, he or she has in some way gained an advantage over us. But this seems intolerable and we must act so as to take the advantage away, to make the criminal suffer and so redress the balance.

Up to now in this chapter I have tried to offer a psychological, or perhaps more accurately a psychodynamic, and specifically a psychoanalytical, explanation of society's urge for retribution [45]. Acceptance of this explanation might go some little way towards loosening the hold which this urge has upon our ways of thinking and feeling. But you don't have to accept it, and you certainly don't need to accept it in order to see that determinism knocks the props from under the idea of retributive punishment – or, to use less colloquial language, deprives it of any rational justification. What, after all, does determinism say about criminals? That their crimes are the end products of long and complex chains of causality. Free will does not exist as some mystical force which breaks into these causal chains in order to sever them at a point just before a crime is committed. It does not create out of nothing some motivation alien to criminals' natures which would make them refrain from the crimes which they are bent upon committing. How could it possibly do so? Such ideas are absurd. And it is demeaning to let them fool us into thinking that retributive punishment is justifiable.

This diatribe, it should again be emphasised, is directed only against punishment which is retributive. Criminals may need to be confined in order to protect the public, to deter them from future crime, to deter others from crime, or even to provide a setting within which reform might be possible. A determinist has no need to quarrel with any of this. But to punish them, or add to their punishment, on the ground that they deserve it because they have somehow failed to make proper use of their free will, is … well, let's call a spade a spade: it's savagery, cruelty. The poet A.E. Housman was a homosexual at a time when homosexuals were abhorred and homosexual conduct was still a crime and, in protest against this, he wrote a poem which began:

> Oh who is that young sinner with the handcuffs on his wrists?
> And what has he been after that they groan and shake their fists?
> And wherefore is he wearing such a conscience-stricken air?
> Oh they're taking him to prison for the colour of his hair.
>
> 'Tis a shame to human nature such a head of hair as his;
> In the good old time 'twas hanging for the colour that it is;
> Though hanging isn't bad enough and flaying would be fair
> For the nameless and abominable colour of his hair.

Long after his death, our society conceded Housman's point. Attitudes have changed. Everyone always knew that people don't create the natural colour of their hair. Nowadays most people know that homosexuals don't create their homosexuality. And some day, perhaps, we shall realise that criminals don't create their criminality either – and that "retributive justice" is a contradiction in terms.

23.

Towards a rational penal system?

Retributive punishment can be justified, if it can be justified at all, only on the basis of free will. Very few people want to give up on retributive punishment and this, no doubt, is one reason why very few people want to give up on free will. It is of course *possible* to be a determinist and still to advocate this kind of punishment, just as it was possible for Lord Chief Justice Goddard to accept the insanity of a murderer and still say that he should have been hanged, but in practice this position would be difficult to sustain.

The title of this chapter is inspired by an interview with the late Roy Jenkins (then not yet Lord Jenkins of Hillhead). When he first became Home Secretary it was thought that his views on crime and punishment might be too liberal for the public's taste, and so the interviewer asked him about them. In reply, he said he wanted a penal system that was *rational*. It was, as might have been expected, an astute response, because although a rational system was the last thing that many people wanted, they couldn't very well object to having one. (Actually, Roy Jenkins said "wational", not rational, because that was the way he spoke, so they tended to mock him for that instead.)

Roy Jenkins, of course, was implicitly rejecting the idea, beloved of the popular press and of the general public, that there are only two positions which can be adopted towards crime: being hard on it and being soft on it; that hardness and softness are measures simply and solely of the severity of punishment; and that hardness works and softness doesn't. There is no room within this simple approach for initiatives which are reformative, remedial, or indeed preventive. To anyone who knows anything at all about crime, and wants actually to reduce it, this misses the point and makes no sense. Measures which people would call "soft" may serve in fact to reduce crime, and measures they would call "hard" may go in fact to increase it. But these things are not acceptable because, for very many people, effectiveness is not really the name of the game: even if the facts were clear to them, they would still demand simply that governments be "hard" on crime.

I don't recall, if I ever knew, exactly what Roy Jenkins meant by "rational", or how rational he thought the system could really become. In a system which made no concessions at all to irrationality, retributive punishment would play no part whatever, but the other aims of sentencing, set out at the start of Chapter 21, would still be relevant. The overriding purpose would simply be the protection of society through the prevention of crime. The focus would be on the harmfulness, rather than the wickedness, of the offender. Imprisonment would still be necessary in very many cases - and in the case of offenders who were both dangerous and unreachable, it might have to last a very long time - but, subject to that, the aim of those involved in the penal system would be to decide on the approach best calculated to turn the offender away from crime. It is here, in relation to the *treatment* of offenders, and not in the hair-splitting statutory rules about deserts and culpability, that their varying mental states would be important. Under our present system, reform of the offender hardly gets a look-in, and our prisons are full of people with mental illness which goes largely untreated. Official statistics tell us that three-quarters of prisoners have below average I.Q.s, that over two-thirds have one or more mental health disorders and that nearly one-tenth are psychotic (that's to say, insane).

The only prison in the country which is run entirely on

therapeutic principles is Grendon. Its regime, far from being soft or lenient, makes much greater demands on the prisoners than any ordinary prison: a consultant psychiatrist uses unexpectedly colourful language in saying [46] that it provides "group therapy with turbo-charged-rocket-boost-high-voltage-plasma-engines, going at warp factor ten". A report by the Chief Inspector of Prisons in 2009 reaffirmed its "remarkable achievements with some of the ... most dangerous and difficult prisoners". It was awarded the Longford Prize in 2008, when the judges described it as a beacon of hope for the prison service. But Grendon's foundation stone was laid by Rab Butler fifty years ago and no answering beacons have as yet been lit. A few of us may remember Lord Macaulay's poem describing the beacons which warned of the Spanish Armada: "All night from tower to tower they sprang; they sprang from hill to hill", till in the end "the red glare on Skiddaw roused the burghers of Carlisle". Nothing like that has happened to Grendon and, far from its ethos being replicated elsewhere, the question now is whether it can be preserved within Grendon itself.

I claim no originality for advocating a system of the kind described in this chapter, because many other people have done so. A name that comes to mind is that of Barbara Wootton, sociologist and criminologist and magistrate among other things, who became the first woman life peer as Baroness Wootton of Abinger. (She kindly invited me to lunch at the House of Lords once although, for reasons not relevant here, the occasion wasn't entirely a success.) She advocated that our present punitive system be replaced by a preventive one, and suggested that the concept of criminal responsibility should be allowed to "wither away" [47]. She didn't make this suggestion because she was an avowed determinist but simply because she thought the concept was amorphous and impossible to pin down. Back in 1968 Barbara Wootton took part in a television debate in the *Your Witness* series. The motion was that "the purpose of the criminal law is, and ought to be, the punishment of wickedness". She opposed this motion, arguing that the purpose of the criminal law ought simply to be the prevention of crime. Do I need to add that most of the "jury" voted against her?

The vote would probably go the same way if the same motion were debated today, and it would be stupid indeed to suppose that a rational, preventive system could be established any time soon. We live in a democracy and even if government ministers wanted to move towards a system of this kind the electorate wouldn't stand for it. Because let's look for a minute at the implications. Earlier in this book mention was made of Myra Hindley, who colluded with her lover Ian Brady in the cold-blooded and horrifying murder of a number of children. How would she be treated under a preventive system from which retributive punishment had been eliminated? My guess – and it is only a guess, but let's assume for the sake of argument that it's right – is that, once her crimes had been discovered and Ian Brady had been taken out of her life, the risk of her committing any more crimes was pretty much non-existent. Looking to the future, she was probably not a harmful person. So if we run through the purposes of sentencing set out at the start of Chapter 21, we see that the only one which would justify a court in sending her to gaol (or doing anything else to her) would be aim (b), in so far as it includes the deterrence of other would-be murderers. This is an aim known to penologists as "general deterrence". It is hard to guess what her sentence would have needed to be in order to achieve that aim, but almost certainly it would not have involved her being kept in prison until she died.

Public opinion would have to move so far as to be hardly visible from where we now stand if this sort of outcome were to become acceptable. Lord Denning, scarcely a liberal-minded man but recently voted, in one of those polls set up to decide such things, the most inspiring lawyer of all time, maintained that the main purpose of sentencing was "denunciation": if the crime were abhorrent, the sentence should express the abhorrence. His view would no doubt be echoed by many other people, but denunciation, in so far as it goes beyond general deterrence, would surely play no part in a rational system, and certainly none in a system which acknowledges the truth of determinism – the truth that criminals commit crimes only because they dangle at the end of a causal chain not of their own making. The idea of denunciation seems to hark back to something mentioned in the previous chapter: the desire, by punishing the offender's wickedness, to shore up our own virtue and keep our own wickedness at bay.

For myself, I am aware of a conflict of feelings. Since I am human, I feel deep anger and deep abhorrence when I think about the sort of crimes in which Myra Hindley took part, and I cannot acquit myself of a desire for vengeance. I often catch myself feeling satisfaction when condign punishment is visited upon some offender who has arrogantly and cruelly broken the rules by which most of us manage to live. But I feel real anger, too, about the way in which, when such criminals are caught, we ignore all the distorting influences which society has allowed to bear upon them, along with any contribution which their genetic endowment has made to their criminality, and treat their crimes, not as a result of these things, but as a result of something called free will. If free will really did allow us to choose our personalities, or to slough them off at will, who in the world would freely choose to have the personality of a serial killer, or to act in accordance with it? Would you choose even to step into the slightly more comfortable shoes of Burglar Bill? Criminals are victims of causality just as their victims are, and none the less so if, as sometimes happens, causality has made them arrogant, gloating and glad to be the people they are.

There is another lesson which determinism teaches us about crime, and that is the need to intervene more often, more early, and more effectively, in the lives of those who are on the way to becoming criminals. Although attempts actually to do this are spasmodic and half-hearted, the need to do it is coming increasingly to be recognised. Even if we profess to reject determinism, we know deep down that our only hope of making a real reduction in crime lies in tackling at an early stage the chains of causality which lead to it. We cannot rely on "free will" to do the job: it will not come riding to the rescue at the last minute, like the U.S. Cavalry in an old Hollywood film. It is true that the imposition of penalties on convicted offenders may deter them from future crime, because it modifies the causal chain, but this comes too late – too late for the criminals and too late for their victims.

PART VI

LAST THOUGHTS

24.

Free will and religion: some parallels

Charles Bradlaugh lived from 1833 to 1891, a great social reformer who disbelieved in God. He was a founder of the National Secular Society, and he was elected Member of Parliament for Northampton but he had difficulty in taking his seat because he wouldn't swear the Oath of Allegiance (it was the swearing to God that he objected to, not the allegiance itself). He was militant in his disbelief and held public meetings at which he took out his pocket watch and invited God, if he existed, to strike him dead within 60 seconds (or three minutes or five minutes: accounts vary). They called him "Bradlaugh the atheist" and it wasn't a kindly description. *Punch* caricatured him as "The Northampton Cherub", a malevolent bat with a devil's tail. Atheism was an aberration and atheists were rebels.

Bradlaugh stood somewhere between our own time, a time in which disbelief in God is widespread and usually attracts no condemnation, and the Age of Faith which existed many centuries ago, an age in which atheism would have been almost unthinkable. There may then have been a few who questioned the existence of God but, by and large, it would not have entered anyone's head to do so. Religious belief was in the air that people breathed, taken for granted. They were born into it, they lived in it and they died in it. They *knew* that God existed, and knew with such certainty that they would never have felt the need to say so. And don't we think now about free will in very much the same way as our ancestors thought then about God? Don't we accept it just as unquestioningly? Our own age may not be an age of religious faith, but it is an age of faith in free will.

Chapter 7 was concerned with the idea that free will is a gift from God and with the contrary idea that God's omniscience precludes the existence of free will. When I started this book I had no intention of saying anything else about religious belief, but as I wrote it I began to see so many parallels between belief in God and belief in free will that I now feel an urge to add this chapter.

One of these parallels lies in the fact that God and free will are both mystical concepts. The idea that we might be able to *understand* God is almost blasphemous: God is by definition transcendent, supernatural, and (as the old hymn has it) moves in a mysterious way his wonders to perform. If an unbeliever questions a believer about the nature or behaviour of God, the unbeliever will be met sooner or later (and probably sooner) by the assertion that, because God is what God is, such questions are unanswerable. And so it is with free will: those who want to live by it must accept that there are no good answers to the questions which they might (but seldom do) ask about its nature and supposed effects. It was Kant who bracketed God and free will, together with immortality, as being beyond the power of the human intellect. And certainly this must, by definition, be true of God and immortality. But ought not free will to be different? Determinism, after all, is a credible alternative, and if we are to go on rejecting determinism in favour of free will, believing in it and living our lives by it, ought we not to know, and to be able to describe and to substantiate, its nature?

Another parallel lies in what might be called the coloured spectacles syndrome. It is sometimes said that optimists see the world through rose coloured spectacles: their emotional outlook colours their view of existence, and the colour in which they see it then goes to confirm and reinforce the emotional outlook which made them see it in that way. People who are depressed, as I happen to know to my cost, see existence through spectacles of a very different kind, ones which give them a vision so terrible that sometimes they will die rather than endure it. Existence is not *really* the way these people see it (or we don't think it is, though who are we to say?) but that's the way it seems to them – the way it *is* for them. And many kinds of emotionally inspired belief may have the same self-validating effect. I suggested in Chapter 19 that those who believe in free will see the behaviour of their fellow human beings in such a way as to justify and reinforce their belief – just as religious believers see the work of God so clearly in the workings of the world that they cannot see these workings in any other way.

For the next parallel we return to a point raised in Chapter 2 but not considered since then. When my generation were school children, we would ask, How did the universe come to exist? The answer would be, God made it. If we were bold, we would then ask, How did God come to exist? But the answer was less clear; perhaps God had always existed ...? But then, perhaps, the universe might always have existed ...? [48] A similar question was raised about free will in Chapter 2: how did that come to exist? But here we cannot give quite the same answer. We can't very well say that free will has always existed, if only because the human race hasn't always existed. It would not be credible to suggest that the earth's first life forms had free will. It would not be credible to suggest that an influenza virus now has free will, or even a tapeworm, or a woodlouse. All these living things must be creatures of causality, governed and moved purely by physical processes. If we, as twenty-first century people, are not governed by physical processes because we have what we call free will, we must have managed, at some stage of our evolution, to detach ourselves from the laws of nature which up until then had governed us. But when and how? So far as I know, evolutionary scientists have not concerned themselves with these questions, and they are unlikely to do so unless they themselves believe in free will, know exactly what it is and manage to devise some criteria according to which its existence or non-existence can be recognised. We would be wise not to hold our breath.

Yet another parallel lies in the fact that, like belief in God, belief in free will (so long as it remains unexamined) tends to be comforting to those who hold it. The Royal Duke's admission recorded in Chapter 15 that, though he had never had doubts about religion, he probably would have had if he had been more intelligent, is one that could be applied equally to free will – but, as I suggested there, it would be equally questionable because our lives are not ruled by reason and we don't, by and large, take intellectual journeys towards destinations which do not attract us.

And the "utilitarian" argument for belief in God – that it ought to be fostered because it is socially cohesive and leads people to live better lives – is paralleled by a similarly utilitarian argument for belief in free will: that it is an important part of our society, our culture, our morality, our sense of self, and so on, and that we must therefore hang on to it however incoherent it may prove, on examination, to be, because humankind cannot stand very much reality. This argument was considered and rejected in Chapter 16. The idea here is that free will is a "necessary fiction", but what *is* the fiction? Even fictions must make some sense (many a novel has been spoilt for me because it turns on a point of law and the author has got it wrong), and free will makes none.

And isn't there a rather strong similarity between the theologians of religion and the philosophers of free will? I went to school with someone who later became a Bishop of the Church of England. He told me once that he had been spending time in his study discarding out of date books on theology. For a moment I was surprised to think that theology could become out of date, but of course it does:

ideas about God are always changing. And his remark brought home to me also the sheer volume of theological writing which the idea of God inspires through the generations – every bit of it mistaken and useless if by any chance God does not exist. Is there not a parallel here between the theologians who engage in the academic discussion of religious doctrine and the philosophers who write in much the same way about free will? Aren't they, too, producing what are really works of theology, seeking to pin down a concept which will always escape them, searching for an intellectual certainty which is not to be had?

And finally there is another parallel. In 1987 *The Times* ran an article by the journalist Bernard Levin in which he attacked the idea of determinism. This brought a response from Dr. Wilfred Beckerman, a fellow of Balliol College, Oxford, and since then a Professor and a distinguished economist. Beckerman's article was a beautifully clear and concise defence of determinism and demolition of free will. Levin made a rather incoherent response, and Beckerman finished the job with another article. I summoned the courage to write and congratulate him, and in a postcard reply he said it was good to have one supporting letter amongst all the hate mail he had received. The point of this story is that attacks on free will, and on the implications of free will, do indeed generate a great deal of anger – just as attacks on God and religion did at the time of Charles Bradlaugh and in earlier times. Nowadays attacks of the latter kind, though not universally well received, are much more acceptable, and it would be good to think that attacks on free will might come in time to be treated in the same way. Having regard to the supernatural character of the God in whom believers believe, it really is impossible to decide upon his existence by means of reason and logic; but it would be very strange if it were not possible to decide by these means upon the existence of free will.

25.

The nonsense of free will

Two philosophers who believe in free will have been named in this book: Immanuel Kant and Professor Robert Kane. Both would be determinists but for one thing, a different thing in each case. Kant (Chapter 17) accepted that the everyday world in which we live is a world of determinism but thought that free will must nonetheless exist, in a way which is (as he would have agreed) literally inexplicable, in the noumenon. Professor Kane (Chapter 11), for his part, pins his faith in free will - albeit a kind of free will which is not free "at the point of delivery" - on the idea of "self-forming actions". If you accept Kant's reasons for thinking that free will exists in the noumenon, well and good. And if you feel convinced by Kane's suggestions about the power of self-forming actions, equally well and good. But bear in mind that if these particular things *don't* stand up to detached examination, and to my mind they certainly don't, then two strong opponents of determinism must be counted among its supporters.

"Determinism" is an off-putting name for a simple everyday process. Maybe (harking back to Chapter 8) determinism has a bit of chance – real inexplicable randomness – mixed in with it, so that when this book refers to determinism it should really be referring to determinism-and-chance. If so, so be it. (Those who live in Chorlton-cum-Hardy call it "Chorlton" and perhaps I can be forgiven for following their example by not adding "and chance" to every mention of determinism.) This conclusion might not be entirely credible or very welcome – if someone says they love you, you don't want to think their statement might be accidental – but both determinism and chance are equally inimical to free will and that is another point to bear in mind.

And, really and truly, the nonsensicality of free will hardly depends upon the validity of either determinism or determinism-and-chance. Free will is nonsensical because it doesn't make sense. There has to be an indissoluble nexus or link between what we see as people's characters and the things they do. Their behaviour tells us about their characters, and our knowledge of their characters tells us what behaviour to expect. (If on occasion they seem to act "out of character", there is always a causal explanation for their unexpected departure, just as there was in Chapter 2 for the unexpected failure of the water to come out of the tap, and they themselves could probably tell you what it was.) If their behaviour were the product of free will, this could not be so. An act done in exercise of free will would be unpredictable and inexplicable. If, because of free will, Burglar Bill decides to turn away from the empty house despite his single-minded motivation to break in, his act would, by definition, be unmotivated. Is there such a thing as an act which is deliberate but unmotivated? No. And if there were wouldn't our perceptions of one another be entirely destroyed? So it isn't a question of whether we can find *room* for free will in a universe otherwise governed by determinism or determinism-and-chance: a sort of "free will of the gaps" akin to the idea of a "God of the gaps" put forward by those who look for God in the diminishing areas of reality which science has yet to explain. It's no good looking for some flaw in the case for determinism, some fault in the argument, some over-simplification, some misdescription, some assumption which is open to question … because however much room you find, and wherever you find it, it can't be filled with something nonsensical.

Let's run briefly through some familiar reactions to any attack on the idea of free will:

"But I *know* I have a *choice* of what to do." Indeed you have. But you make the choice you make because you are the person you are: would you want it otherwise? And you are the person you are because of the influences which have shaped you: how could you not be?

"But I want my actions to be *up to me.*" Of course you do and so they are. But the "me" they're up to is the product of a chain of causality which then runs on into what you do. Is that so bad? How could it not be so?

"But I believe in *evil* and *wickedness.*" By all means label some acts in that way if you want to, but the labelling doesn't prevent them from having causal explanations like any other acts. And by all possible means feel free to believe in *goodness* and *virtue* as well: causality has created them, too, but we are right to celebrate them.

"And I believe in *responsibility*". Well, we must all believe strongly in the necessity of holding people responsible and in inculcating feelings of responsibility. Isn't that enough? Come right down to it, what more is there?

In the course of its long evolutionary history, the human race has held and later discarded many beliefs. For the most part, these beliefs seemed to our ancestors to explain things for which they had no other explanation, about themselves or about the outside world. The explanations they gave tended to be magical ones: they wouldn't have stood up to rational examination and they didn't include an explanation of how the magic itself came into existence, but because magic is by its nature inexplicable that didn't seem to matter.

Early beliefs in a multiplicity of gods – the deities of nature, the gods of sun and moon, the more personal gods in whom the Romans and the Greeks believed – are obvious examples. (In a remarkable essay called *Memorial Service* [49], the great American journalist H.L Mencken set out the names of some 185 gods, adding: "They were gods of the highest standing and dignity – gods of civilised peoples – worshipped and believed in by millions. All were theoretically omnipotent, omniscient, and immortal. And all are dead.") Beliefs of this kind were illusory, and we no longer have them. In our western culture, such primitive religious beliefs have been replaced by monotheism - belief in a single god - although the identity and nature of the single god may be in dispute (and this belief, too, may be a magical belief, but this isn't the place to argue about that).

Other examples are belief in the devil and in witches who were thought to be in league with him: although these beliefs seemed in the past to be completely justified, they seemed so only because they served a psychological purpose for us, and most people have ceased to project their own unrecognised feelings into these entities. Although there are, sadly, some peoples, in parts of Africa for example, who still hold to a belief in witches and, still more sadly, act on this belief, we in our part of the world have mostly discarded it. But unless the human race manages to destroy itself in the fairly near future, our evolution – and particularly the evolution of our ideas – is not over yet, and who can doubt that there are more magical beliefs yet to be discarded?

Belief in free will is surely one of these. It has all the necessary characteristics. It is not hard to understand why it should have become embedded in the human psyche, because it serves a number of purposes for us. Some would argue, as we've already noticed, that, whether the concept makes sense or not, we must maintain our belief in it as a matter of practical necessity (Chapter 16). We must continue to inculcate it in our children, so it is said, because it fosters good behaviour, underpins our sense of responsibility, forms an integral part of our morality, supports our social institutions, and so on. But doesn't human progress depend upon our willingness to see things as they really are; and wouldn't it be humiliating if our civilisation were really to depend upon maintaining and promulgating false beliefs?

And let's not forget that belief in free will, though it may perhaps have had some desirable results, has also given us an excuse for inflicting a great deal of unjustifiable cruelty. The belief that if someone inflicts on us a *hurt* of some kind, that person is to blame for doing so, and deserves to *suffer* for it, is firmly built into us. It is very primitive. When, as a young child, I hit my head on some inanimate object, I was encouraged to hit it back. This act, often accompanied by an adult cry of (for example), "Naughty table", certainly relieved my feelings; and very many childhoods must be punctuated by such events. And so may some adult lives: no one who has seen it will forget the image of John Cleese in *Fawlty Towers* beating his car with a tree branch when it let him down once too often. In medieval times animals – chickens, rats, field mice, pigs – were actually put on trial, prosecuted and punished for "crimes" which took the form of damage done to human beings or their property [50]. Incredibly, some were burned, hanged, buried alive or put on the rack. They were simply doing what animals are programmed to do, following their natural propensities, so this kind of punishment could hardly have been inflicted on them unless they had been credited, explicitly or implicitly, with the ability to transcend their natures – in other words, with some kind of free will. To us, the whole thing seems absurd as well as cruel. Perhaps our descendants will come to see that the *retributive* punishment which we inflict on one another is little different from hitting a table, beating a car, or hanging a pig.

In this book I've tried to suggest that we could manage perfectly well to live without a belief in free will. We certainly shouldn't have to forgo or to repudiate our natural feelings. These feelings might be leavened in certain ways, in the light of a rejection of free will, particularly in our attitudes towards those who are so built as to differ from us, whether in their criminal or anti-social propensities, in their religious beliefs, or in other ways. But surely our civilisation would be enhanced, rather than endangered, by this. Freud said [51], "Civilisation consists in progressive renunciation." Some renunciations are hard, but they are still worthwhile and in the end they are surely unavoidable.

I have a friend who was brought up in the Jewish faith. He thought a lot about free will and found it a completely incoherent concept. But he was in a painful predicament because his religion required him to accept it. A little later, and quite suddenly, he lost his religious faith and was relieved to realise that this allowed him also to stop believing in free will. He was glad to be rid of this belief. So am I, and so are many other people – how many I've no idea, but I suspect that the number is growing – and I doubt whether any of us has suffered any adverse consequences as a result of our disbelief. There is, on the contrary, some satisfaction to be had in renouncing the fairy tale of free will and embracing the reality of determinism – some satisfaction and paradoxically, as my friend discovered, a sense of freedom too. It is after all, as the Gospel according to St. John tells us (8:32), the truth that makes you free.

So I come back to my beginning. We really do act the way we do because we are the people we are. Don't we? And we really haven't made ourselves the people we are. Have we? And when you try the slot machine, does the penny drop and do you see determinism?

26.

Beyond determinism?

A thought which surfaced fleetingly in the previous chapter is one that I should like to pin down and try to develop. Perhaps I can approach this task by way of something like Wittgenstein's ladder. The philosopher Ludwig Wittgenstein came to Trinity College, Cambridge, in the early twentieth century. I think it was he who introduced himself to Bertrand Russell, who was already there, by handing him a piece of paper on which were written the words: "The statement on the other side of this paper is false". Russell turned the paper over and found the same words written on the other side. Conceivably it wasn't Wittgenstein who did this, and certainly it has nothing to do with his ladder, but it makes a good story.

Wittgenstein's ladder appears towards the end of his *Tractatus Logico-Philosophicus* [52]. Translated from the German, he says:

> My propositions are elucidatory in this way: he who understands me finally recognises them as senseless, when he has climbed out through them, on them, over them. (He must so to speak throw away the ladder, after he has climbed up on it.)

I suppose it is *determinism* which in some sense I want to throw away. This isn't because what I have said about it is senseless (oh, no), but because determinism itself is somehow not the *point*. The real point is the self-contradictory nature of free will.

The philosopher mentioned in Chapter 14 wrote a book called *Free Will* and devoted it, perhaps paradoxically, to a consideration of determinism. Free will itself didn't really come into his picture. He was concerned only to show that there is no "logical bar" to free will. Similarly, the neuroscientist Benjamin Libet (Chapter 9) seems to have assumed that if only he could show that human acts were initiated by the conscious mind he would have succeeded in preserving free will. These are just two examples of the way in which many philosophers and scientists, along with nearly all the rest of us, take it for granted that the idea of free will is so self-evidently sensible and coherent that there is no need to question or analyse it, while determinism is a strange idea and a Bad Thing against which all available weapons of critical analysis must be directed. I have railed against this attitude several times, and I hope I may be forgiven for railing once again. The truth surely is that if they summoned up only half as much of the energy which they devote to the critical examination of determinism and devoted it to an objective analysis of free will, then free will would fall apart in their hands and determinism would cease to seem important. As it is, they are failing to see the wood for the trees.

Disbelievers in free will have a problem. The only road down which we are allowed to go in order to justify our disbelief is a road signposted to "determinism". In the book just mentioned, the philosopher commits himself unequivocally to three assertions. One, that free will is a live issue only for philosophers. I hope this isn't so: if it is, then I've wasted my time in writing this book. Two, that it is an issue for them only because of the determinist argument. This may very well be so, and that's exactly what I'm complaining about. And three, that to *meet* the determinist argument is of itself to establish the freedom of the will. But this really is not so. No, no, no, it really is not. Meeting the determinist argument wouldn't give you free will: it would give you indeterminacy, it would just leave you floundering. You can't establish free will merely by getting rid of determinism. You need to do something more. You need to make sense of it, show what it is, show how it works.

So let us summon up our courage and kick away the determinist ladder. Although it has served a useful purpose in getting us to where we are, we shall forget all about determinism for the moment and look only at free will. Let us just remind ourselves of some very obvious truths.

"What a piece of work is a man!", says Hamlet [53]. What a piece of work. Of *work*. Think what goes into the *making* of us. Remember first that the people we become depends a great deal on our hereditary endowment and that this comes to us from our parents. "Choose your parents carefully", the old joke has it. But we don't. Nor do we ask to be born. Life is thrust upon us: we have no say in the matter. Before we are conceived, we do not exist, and when we are born we are products of the genes of other people. And remember, too, that we emerge from the womb into an all-embracing but changing environment which, though not of our making, is going to interact with this hereditary endowment and mould the personalities which, at every stage of our journey through life, we possess. Pause for a moment on this word "environment": how inadequate it is to describe not just the physical world, or our part of it, not just the people who live there, and especially the all-important ones who are close to us, but the whole wealth of culture, discovery, knowledge, understanding, attitudes and values which come to us down the centuries, which exist at our birth, which develop as we live our lives and which affect us all, to a greater or lesser degree, directly or indirectly, in one way or another, as we grow up.

This is how we are made, how we come to be, how we come to be the people we are. It is this that produces us. It is of this that we are products, right from the moment of our conception to the moment when that which drew from out the boundless deep turns again home. Change the details of any part of this constituent process and we should (slightly or not so slightly) be different people behaving differently. And remember also that it would be impossible for anyone to have a meaningful relationship with anyone else unless the behaviour of each of them were a manifestation of their personality and showed them for the people they are. According to the Gospel of St. Matthew (7:20), "by their fruits ye shall know them": and this aphorism deserves an emphasis not only on "fruits" but also on "know", because in truth no one could ever be said to *know* anybody if their behaviour told us nothing about them.

Does anyone seriously disagree with anything in the last two paragraphs? Have I done anything more than say a few things that are obviously true? I haven't used the D word, and many (including the philosopher who wrote the book) would say that I haven't painted a picture of determinism. And most people would say that they could agree with what I've said without having to call themselves determinists. But if my picture is an accurate one, what room does it leave for anything called free will? If an act done by Eloise (who is another character hanging around and waiting to be invented) is the product of her personality and, because of that, it tells us something about her, how could it at the same time be done free from that personality and from the forces which have created it? If it *were* free then it might have been a quite different act, and then it would tell us nothing about her and we couldn't ask why she did it.

You don't need explicitly to accept determinism – a determinism which perhaps still seems to you an unwelcome, arid, scientific doctrine – in order to see that free will makes no sense. A simple acceptance of the human condition is enough to do the job. The way (recorded in Chapter 1) in which I framed my own early vision of determinism, *a person acts as he does because he is what he is; and he has not made himself what he is,* is perhaps more a simple statement of an obvious state of affairs than a strict description of determinism. And it is no doubt in an attempt to escape from the consequences of this state of affairs – because there can be no other means of escape – that some philosophers have come up with the idea of an "originator". The suggestion is that our heredity and environment have somehow built into us a capacity to detach ourselves from that very heredity and environment in order to do things which are not products of the personalities which heredity and environment have given us. We looked briefly at this idea in Chapter 3, and surely it merits no more than a brief look – partly because it is so absurd, and partly because, even if it were in some way valid, it wouldn't actually serve to resurrect free will. If Eloise's act were produced by her originator, you would still have to ask the questions posed at the end of the last paragraph, and there would still be no good answers. After all … what *is* this entity called Eloise? She is a product of circumstance, a creation of natural laws, and so would be her originator if she had one.

The real point, the all-important point which is so often ignored, is not that we are of determinism's making (although we are), but that we are not and cannot be of our *own* making. And the idea of free will founders not because of determinism but because it makes not the slightest bit of sense.

Epilogue

Samuel Butler's *Erewhon* [54] was mentioned in Chapter 3. Imagine that you, like his protagonist, come unexpectedly upon a new country in which, strangely, the inhabitants speak English. Let's call it Erewhesle.

One of the most notable characteristics of the people of Erewhon was that they hated and feared machines, thinking that they would evolve to the point of challenging human supremacy, and all their more complicated machines had been destroyed long ago. In Erewhesle, by contrast, they love machines, and the more complicated the better. The intelligence of the Erewheslians far outstrips our own, and the intelligence of their Professor Zog far outstrips that of any other Erewheslian. Professor Zog has devoted many years to constructing a machine so complex that he has not yet dared to show it to anyone else. Armed with the most profound understanding of computer science he has built a computerised robot which behaves just like a human being. Not content with that, he has nurtured his robot for twenty years or so, refining it, subjecting it to influences and events similar to those which human beings encounter in the course of their lives, so that it has come, in his view, to behave not just like a human being, but like an adult, mature, experienced human being.

By means on which we need not speculate, you obtain an introduction to Professor Zog and persuade him to show you his robot. In fact you carry on a prolonged conversation with it, and if you closed your eyes you could easily suppose that you were conversing with an intelligent and rather charming human being. You then have a discussion with Zog himself, conducted in private so as not to offend the robot. He is immensely proud of his creation: he believes that its brain replicates all human characteristics, and he is confident that, once he puts it into the public domain, it will win him a Lebon Prize. You then find yourself saying, "Ah, but does it have free will?".

Zog looks blank, and it transpires that the people of Erewhesle, for all their intelligence, have no knowledge of the concept of free will. Zog is so crestfallen that you make light of this shortcoming and do not like to press the point. But Zog insists:

"Please," he says, "don't sell me short. If my computerised robot lacks some human characteristic, I can modify it. Only tell me what that characteristic is, what it does, how it works."

"Well …," you begin.

"Oh," says Zog, "I know what it might be. You've seen those little round balls which your National Lottery uses to make a random selection of the winning numbers? The way they whirl about in the machine and come out one by one?" (How does he know about this? We won't ask.) "Is that the sort of effect free will produces? I suppose I could reproduce something like that, but why …?" and he trails off.

"No, no," you say, quoting a little bit of T.S. Eliot which happens to be among the snippets of poetry which have lodged in your mind, "That was not what I meant at all. That was not it, at all."

Zog misses the allusion, as one might expect, but he takes your correction in good part:

"O.K.," he says, "that's not free will. So, please, tell me what it is."

And he leans back in his chair with an expectant expression and an encouraging smile.

Notes

GENERAL NOTE. References in this book to laws and institutions are to those of England and Wales.

1. Michael Brooks, *13 Things That Don't Make Sense* (Profile Books, 2009), p. 152.
2. It was of course Adolf Hitler's demand that Germans should have more *lebensraum*, or living space, which led to the expansionist aspirations of Nazi Germany and thus to the Second World War.
3. Stephen Hawking and Leonard Mlodinow in *The Grand Design* (Bantam Press, 2010), p. 5, famously declare that "philosophy is dead", justifying this by adding: "Philosophy has not kept up with modern developments in science, particularly physics". This seems to imply a rather narrow view of philosophy, but it does illustrate the way in which scientists and philosophers may contend for the same ground.
4. Ted Honderich, *Philosopher: A Kind of Life* (Routledge, 2001), p. 17.
5. Albert Einstein, *Science, Philosophy and Religion* from Einstein's *Out of My Later Years*, pp 26-29, quoted in Christopher Hitchens (ed.), *The Portable Atheist* (Da Capo Press, 2007), p. 161.
6. Pierre Simon Laplace, *A Philosophical Essay on Probabilities*, translated (Dover Publications, New York, 1951), p. 4.
7. Albert Einstein, in response to a child who had written to him in 1936 to ask if scientists pray, from *Albert Einstein, the Human Side*, p. 32, quoted in Christopher Hitchens' book cited in note 5 above, p. 159.
8. Burglar Bill first appeared in a poem written in 1888 "for the young reciter" by Thomas Anstey Guthrie, using the pseudonym "F. Anstey" under which he also wrote *Vice Versa*. His Burglar Bill later became a character in children's stories by Allan and Janet Ahlberg.
9. Both aphorisms quoted in Robert Kane (ed.) *Free Will* (Blackwell Publishing, 2002), p. 9.

10. Included in Freud, *Some Character-Types Met with in Psycho-Analytic Work*, 1916.
11. Ernest Jones, *Sigmund Freud: Life and Work* (Hogarth Press, 1957), vol. I, pp. 400-401, and vol. II, p. 314. See also Peter Gay, *Freud: A Life For Our Time* (J.M. Dent & Sons, 1988), p. 119:

> In [Freud's] view of the mind, every event, no matter how accidental its appearance, is as it were a knot in intertwined causal threads that are too remote in origin, large in number, and complex in their interaction to be readily sorted out. True: to secure freedom from the grip of causality is among mankind's most cherished, and hence most tenacious, illusory wishes. But Freud sternly warned that psychoanalysis should offer such illusory fantasies no comfort. Freud's theory of the mind is therefore strictly and frankly deterministic.

12. Ted Honderich, *How Free Are You?* (Oxford University Press, 2002), 2nd edn., p. 47.
13. Samuel Butler, *Erewhon or Over the Range* (Heron Books edition, 1969), pp. 91-92.
14. Alan Wood, *Bertrand Russell: The Passionate Sceptic* (George Allen & Unwin, 1957), p. 156.
15. Voltaire (pen name of Francois Marie Arouet, 1694-1778), *Philosophical Dictionary*, published 1764.
16. For such understanding of this subject as I have acquired, I am mainly indebted to Manjit Kumar, *Quantum* (Icon Books, 2009). Authority is to be found there for statements in this and the next paragraph.
17. For a popular account of Libet's experiments, see the book cited in note 1 above, pp. 151-163. They are dealt with in many other places – e.g., Daniel C. Dennett, *Freedom Evolves* (Penguin Books, 2003).
18. Marcus du Sautoy, *The Times*, 21 October 2009.
19. For an entertaining treatment, see Colin McGinn, *The Making of a Philosopher* (Scribner, 2002), pp. 178-186.
20. The reference is to the character, a scientist and former Nazi, played by Peter Sellers in Stanley Kubrick's 1964 film, *Dr. Strangelove or: How I Learned to Stop Worrying and Love the Bomb*.
21. Book cited in note 12 above, p. 119.

22. Book cited in note 9 above. For Professor Kane's contribution, see pp. 222-248.
23. *The Times*, 12 December 2009.
24. *The Times* Law Report, 8 May 2009.
25. The Human Rights Act was of course enacted by Parliament. Contrary to popular belief, the only function of the Courts is to interpret and apply it as best they can.
26. *The Times*, 29 December 2011.
27. *Radio Times*, 14-20 March 2009, p. 89.
28. Graham McFee, *Free Will* (Acumen, 2000).
29. Book cited in note 28 above, p. 47.
30. One of the "light bulb" jokes may be apposite here. "How many psychotherapists does it take to change a light bulb?" "Only one, but the bulb must want to change."
31. Bryan Magee, *Confessions of a Philosopher* (Weidenfeld & Nicolson, 1997), p. 159. I am mainly indebted to this book for my description of Kant's views on free will. The original edition (cited above) was withdrawn because of a libel action by Ralph Schoenman, who was (to put it mildly) Bertrand Russell's amanuensis in his later years. Magee described him as "an appallingly sinister figure, like an evil dwarf out of Wagner's *Ring*", but the libel action was based on something else which Magee had said about him and which it might be unwise to repeat.
32. Book cited in note 12 above, p. 145.
33. Book cited in note 4 above, pp. 398-399.
34. Book cited in note 4 above.
35. An English translation might be: "To understand is to forgive. To understand everything is to forgive everything."
36. Or, "To understand everything makes one very indulgent".
37. *Proceedings of the British Academy* 48: 1-25.
38. The book is the one cited in note 1 above. The review is in the *Sunday Times*, Culture Section, 15 February 2009, p. 40.
39. Edward Glover, *The Roots of Crime* (Imago, 1960), p. 7.
40. Book cited in note 39 above, p. 24, quoting von Behring.
41. Book cited in note 39 above, p. 8.
42. Franz Alexander and Hugo Staub, *The Criminal, the Judge and the Public* (The Free Press, Illinois, and The Falcon's Wing Press, 1956), p. 30.

43. Richard Hunter and Ida Macalpine (eds.) *Three Hundred Years of Psychiatry 1535 –1860* (Oxford University Press, 1963), p. 75. The accused was one Marie Glovers and, happily, she was not hanged but sentenced to be imprisoned for a year and to "stand on the pillory, and confess this her trespass". The judge was Lord Anderson and his judgment continued:

There is no man here, can speake of [witches] more than my selfe; fewe of them would confesse it, som of them did; against whom proofes were nothing so manifest, as against those that denyed it. They have on their bodies divers strange markes, at which (as som of them have confessed) the Devill suck their bloud; for they have forsaken god, renounced their baptisme, and vowed their service to the Divill; and so the sacrifice which they offer him is their bloud. This woman hath the like markes, on sundry places of her body … Divines, Phisitions, I know they are learned & wise, but to say this is naturall, and tell me neither the cause nor the Cure of it, I care not for your Judgement ….

44. There are of course many similar definitions of projection. This one comes from Anthony Storr, *Human Aggression* (Allen Lane The Penguin Press, 1968), p. 94.
45. I regret the use of these technical terms. Someone wondered whether this "psychological" explanation of the need for retributive punishment was purely a speculation of my own and I am anxious to dispel any such idea.
46. *The Howard Journal of Criminal Justice: Fifty Years of HMP Grendon* (Wiley Blackwell, December 2010), p. 506.
47. Barbara Wootton, *Crime and the Criminal Law (The Hamlyn Lectures)* (Stevens, 1963).
48. The idea that the universe sprang into being spontaneously, and did so as one of many universes (as suggested, e.g., in the book cited in note 3 above), was not current at this time.
49. H.L. Mencken, *Memorial Service*, reproduced in Christopher Hitchens' book, cited in note 5 above, pp. 143-146.
50. See, e.g., Julian Barnes, *A History of the World in 10 and a half Chapters* (Picador, 1990), Chapter 3. The fullest account is thought to be E.P.

Evans, *The Criminal Prosecution and Capital Punishment of Animals* (E.P. Dutton & Company, New York, 1906; reprint edition, The Law Book Exchange, 2009).

51. The first book cited in note 11 above, vol. III, p. 359.
52. Published in German 1921, and in English 1922.
53. *Hamlet*, Act II, scene 2.
54. See note 13 above.

Richard Oerton qualified as a solicitor in 1959. He has been book review editor of the Howard Journal and has worked both in private practice, in legal publishing and at the Law Commission. He has written and edited legal textbooks, and written two non-legal books.